MY
self

AN AUTOBIOGRAPHY OF SURVIVAL

BY KELLEY KITLEY

My Self © 2017 Kelley Kitley

ISBN-10: 1544864817
ISBN-13: 9781544864815

I have tried to recreate events, locales and conversations from my memories of them. In order to maintain their anonymity in some instances I have changed the names of individuals and places.

First Edition

Book cover and interior design by Lynn Rawden
Cover typeset in Playfair Display and Bodoni, interior pages typeset in Bembo

To my husband and my children—my strength.

I didn't choose my imperfections, but I have learned that these imperfections are what make us beautiful.

Dedicated to the women who are beautifully imperfect.

CONTENTS

I

MEMORIES

I ntense heat from the cement of the Chicago street radiates through
the white rubber soles of my new Nike Air Force Ones. It's still hot,
Labor Day just passed; nevertheless, the day is no different from any other
school day. I can still see my friends, almost skipping with pure exhilaration
alongside me, all of us forming the Burling Street Gang, on our daily trek
home from school, usually stopping at the dimly lit bar fully loaded with
a plethora of antique paraphernalia: the vintage Schwinn, spokes rusty and
Cheeto stains on the torn leather handlebar grip, dangling proudly from
the ceiling; old Coke signs draping the walls like upholstery; and mirrors,
some clean, some hazy, some cracked, hung sporadically throughout.

We were, without question, a Coke family—with a generous splash
of rum.

Nothing was more comforting to me than the smiling band of regulars perched like Cheers characters on their self-assigned bar stools, drinks
in hand, condensation dripping on to their hands and their sleeveless,

sun-branded arms. They greeted us like family. They were family—a family smelling like stale beer, booze, and buttery, salted popcorn.

And the word *family* always assured a solid game of pool.

The bar enhanced my love for music, too; hell, it enhanced everything and always filled me with excitement when I got to choose my favorites on the juke box.

Saturdays and Sundays were just regular childhood days. In hindsight, however, those *regular days* created a balance of sorts. I can still smell the freshly cut grass, feel the languor of innocent, innocuous days outdoors basking in unfettered freedom roller skating up and down our street until sunset, flying past house after house, the wind drying our sweaty, watermelon-stained tank tops. We ran through the sprinkler, seeking remedy from the Chicago sun. Al, my dad, empathized and opened with a wrench the bright red fire hydrant directly in front of the bar, and he blasted us. The regulars poked their heads out to watch. We made what seemed to us kids an immense amount of money at our lemonade stand because the bar's patrons were our patrons. I can still taste the cool, citrusy tang; my friends reproved me for drinking the profit. I was happy Kelley, "the girl whose parents own the tavern down the street."

I grew up in Lincoln Park, an up and coming neighborhood of Chicago, in the 1980s. The block was diverse, ranging from single parent to multiracial to same sex families, and everyone drank at our bar.

For several years, Al, my mom Fluff, my two younger siblings, and I lived above the bar in the first home holding memories readily recalled by the irresistible smell of fresh popcorn or by a song, Pat Benatar's *Hit Me With Your Best Shot:* on starry nights, I gazed dreamily out an upstairs window in wonderment at the black firmament, and I pressed my ear to the brown, shag carpet floor pounding with the vibrating jukebox, and I lip-synched to Pat Benatar with youthful rock and roll attitude. The aroma of buttery popcorn and of cigarette smoke seeped upward through the floorboards and through the heating vents.

Despite these sweet evenings, I didn't form too much of an attachment to that particular home above the bar. As our family grew, we moved laterally, buying the "two flat graystone" next door and renting the apartments above the bar to other family members. The bar was home, not the apartments above it and not the "graystone" next door, because 'home' was the smell of booze and the jingle of ice. The rattle of a stainless steel cocktail shaker was the comforting and familiar hallmark of home. By the time I turned eight, the oldest North Side neighborhood bar in Chicago had become my normal and the normal for several regulars making it a primary past-time in their lives. The majority considered themselves extended family, meeting at those designated barstools after their own Thanksgiving or Christmas dinners. Tragically, several had short lives due to drugs and alcohol. Their drinking buddies, their partners in crime, gathered there to solemnly mourn their passing. My favorite was Bad, Bad, Leroy Brown who played the bass at a blues bar up the street. He absolutely was "the baddest man in the whole damn town," his trademark a slow drag on his menthol Kool cigarette just before shooting a hard game of pool. His skin tight jeans revealed a gigantic-looking package, and his tightly tucked turtleneck was equally snug; custom made cowboy boots and a wide-brimmed hat completed the sartorial ensemble. He always called me by name, a shiny gold tooth sparkling in his smile…

★ ★ ★

I'm the eldest of five—two boys, three girls, each of us three years apart. Mondays through Saturdays were our days, but Sundays were "Al days." We visited many venues throughout the day, and my favorite was a high end sports club. The reek of the chlorine- loaded pool still reminds me of a phrase that sticks: *I pity the fool.*

Mr. T from the A-Team swam freestyle, water sliding over his smooth head and down his back, layers of gold glitter hanging from his neck and flashing constantly as he gracefully turned his body side to side, gliding from one end of the almost Olympic-sized pool to the other. He would peek mid-glide over his tree trunk-sized neck to dare me to race him. I always readily accepted the challenge.

He allowed me to win, naturally: "I pity the fool," he'd say, and I laughed with him.

Time in the hot tub was my reward for winning; there, I reveled in my victory. A sign said "Adults Only," but Al victoriously dunked heavy, fluffy, snow white towels in the steamy, bubbling water and cocooned us in them, splaying us in warm splendor on the wet tile, all hypnotized by the gurgling sauna while he massaged our feet like Jesus. He knew how to navigate his way around rules and regulations!

The hot tub ended too soon, and we were off to our next routine Sunday Al adventure. After changing out of wet suits, we speed walked to meet our knight in shining armor, who waited patiently by the ice cream vending machine into which we inserted dollar bills and selected our favorite novelty. Then we piled into Al's chariot, a white Cadillac convertible, and let the wind dry our hair during the ride to the Rock & Roll McDonalds.

Today, seeing a shiny Cadillac symbol transports me to that ride. I can still feel the metal emblem embedded in the canvas, pressing into the back of my thighs while I perched proudly on the back ledge, top down, and ordered through a speaker. I believed with deep conviction that I was the luckiest kid in town. When Al was in a good mood, I *was* the luckiest kid in town, able to persuade him to buy me *anything* I wanted. There seemed to have been no limits.

That feeling of safety I felt around Al changed gradually around age ten into a type of heart-sinking feeling, a hollowness hitting me in the stomach, when I realized he might not be the man I thought him to be. Instead, he began to seem hazardous, like a danger sign, the type of duplicitous man who would set up a dangerous scenario—just so that *he* could be the one to save me.

Riding our bikes to the lagoon to feed the geese seemed a harmless adventure until Dad, disregarding *verboten* signs, as usual, suggested we feed the fowls the popcorn he had told us to load up from the bar. I had just noticed large *Please do not feed the animals* signs everywhere, when a large goose violently grabbed the bottom of my shirt and pulled me into deep, murky water. I panicked and shredded my voice box with my loud screams. That was my first clue that daredevil Al might not be the safe harbor I had once thought him to have been.

The older I got, the riskier his adventures became.

During a winter storm just outside Chicago, he tied my saucer with a rope to the back of a snowmobile and proceeded to drag me down the hill like Evil Knievel. I slammed into a tree and was pretty beaten up. Still, I preferred to believe that despite those risky outings, his intentions were pure.

I'd like to believe that—I still *try* to believe that.

My memories are like an ocean, arriving in waves, the larger the wave, the more vivid the memory. The ones still assaulting me are hulking Hawaiian waves, like the time Al recklessly sped us through the Lincoln

Park Zoo one afternoon on our bikes. What I felt at the time was high anxiety intensified by the mania of his rush around the clock. He was always in a hurry to finish an activity to get somewhere else, although he rarely had anywhere else to be. I recall an animal that had dots, or maybe a lion, a few birds, random families, a screaming child, my dirty shoelaces, and harried two second breaks to slurp my melting Firecracker popsicle while also trying to catch my breath. The only tiny dividend derived from the zoo adventure? Visiting the wishing fountain at the flower house, where my wish never wavered. I squeezed that penny so tight in the palm of my hand and kissed my knuckles. As I threw it into the water, I wished that my crush of the month would love me back. Then we had to go: Al had a fear of crowds.

We made it to our destination, a crowd free-zone for Al, and parked the bikes and raced barefoot through the open grass field to the Von Schiller statue. First one to touch it got an Al dollar.

★ ★ ★

Mom and Al liked to party. The word *party* can refer to many things. Back then, it was at times positive, but often for Mom and Al, ended up terribly negative.

By 1983, Mom and Al owned several bars, restaurants, and nightclubs throughout Chicago—a time when I became increasingly more gregarious, loud, *entertaining,* and attention-seeking. One of the restaurants had a DJ booth. I'd beg to climb up and sing into the microphone while gazing down at all the patrons seated at tables assembled in a boxing ring.

On many nights, our house was infiltrated by friends and family gathering in the kitchen, smoking and drinking, filling the place with noise, and often I was the entertainment in my fleece-footed pajamas and my blonde, bowl haircut.

Al stood and in a robust voice announced, "Ladies and gentlemen, here she is, the one and only Kelley Martel, singing *Baby Face.*"

Apparently, I had been named after a cognac my parents were drinking during conception. At least, that's what Al liked to tell me; actually, it was Mom's middle name.

A brush in one hand and smiling widely, I sang my heart out. Al critiqued my performance, and if it wasn't good *enough,* suggested I try again louder and with more *expression.* The criticism never bothered me; I craved it, because I wanted to get it just right because I loved his attention. I loved all attention—and I wanted more.

Later that night, while the party subsided and the noise lessened, I fell asleep on Al's chest, lulled by his vibrating voice and by the music in the background when he took over the entertainment by telling outrageous stories about the business. Next morning, I awoke in my bed, went downstairs and sat down to a lifeless bowl of sugary cereal and a lukewarm glass of milk Al had left on the kitchen table the night before. This was my cue to *fend for yourself.*

Besides, he needed to *sleep in*—a sleeping pattern that became routine as years progressed. Mom was always the primary parent in the morning but was usually preoccupied with tending to the youngest child's needs. The lack of attention I received the next day compared to the robust attention on drinking nights resulted in a new norm, begging to stay at a friend's house—at times, on more nights than just one or even two. Bottom line? Nursing their hangovers were priority.

I now understand how they felt, the pounding headache, the dry mouth, the nausea, the dire need to sleep. I also remember how I felt. I needed to deflect life. Sheer focus on appearance became a welcome distraction. Hours spent curling my bangs and spraying endless quantities of aerosol hair spray in my probably already lacquered hair consumed over an hour of my daily deflection exercises. The hissing noise from the can, as I sprayed strategically in invisible circles, lines, or in the air, became hypnotic. I was transfixed to the point of missing the school bus occasionally—rather, of allowing my brother and me both to miss the school bus, resulting in Al's fury. He and Mom called a cab, because they were simply just too hungover and unable to drive us to school. On that particular *taxi day,* my brother decided he was petrified of the driver, and Al handed him a butcher knife for his backpack *just in case.* Maybe the intention was to calm my brother or to instill fear, or maybe our dad just wanted to get us the hell out of the house so that he could resume sleeping. Either way, the lesson was learned. We never missed the bus again, but anxiety remained high throughout our morning routine until we stepped onto that big yellow bus at the end of the street.

On the flip side, my parents missed my sports games. As much as I needed them to support me by attending summer softball and winter basketball, Al mentioned that I was no all- star player and would never get much playing time, anyway. I was always told, "We'll be there *next time.*" If I had the lead in a school play, however, he made sure to sit in the front row. Broken promises and inconsistencies were a consistent theme in our household.

I I

A L

I see him in a warm, fuzzy fleece zippered jacket, t-shirtless, exposing his shaved chest. The bitter Chicago winds howl in the background as I watch him embark upon his body perfecting exercise ritual. I can also see him in summer in thin, side-scooped, black running shorts and in gray New Balance running shoes, shirtless in the oppressive Chicago humidity. I can still see him and smell him, sweating cologne, in his favorite Hawaiian shirt, loosely buttoned, lightening bugs glowing in the grass, stars decorating the sky, greedily guzzling cocktails with his girlfriend of the month in our backyard. On a special occasion, he dressed up, donning his gold pinky ring, gold necklace, hoop earring in his left ear, and a straw hat. He was obsessed with body image and imagery. He exuded Old Spice Cologne while sweating profusely. Ladies and Gentlemen . . . my dad . . .

He loved fiction, not in the literary sense but in the true life sense. The blurred line between reality and fantasy was obscure; for example, he repeatedly told us that Tony Danza was a college classmate, creating this fantasy to somehow connect with his children, knowing that *Who's The Boss* and *Taxi* were among our most treasured network shows. He told us to embellish our stories, the most effective way to capture one's "intrigue," his exact words, *It keeps people more interested.* If we told a story he found boring, he interrupted to say we were taking too long or would abruptly say, *Next,* cueing us to move on because he was done listening.

Perhaps it was attention seeking, or a longing to belong, or maybe the narcissistic belief he could get away with his own perception of reality. But who knows, maybe he was right on some level; maybe fantasy is more enticing, thrilling, for a while, but fantasy is a tricky thing. It tends to become problematic, made of hot air and of non-tangibles that either dissolve or come crashing down one way or another. I've observed too many of his male friendships crumble because of this.

I later found out that Al had never attended college, so no Tony Danza, an absolute fabrication. I, too, have been known for exaggeration, a learned behavior. I have to catch myself to return to reality from the effortless slide in the wrong direction, a direction that becomes *the known.*

Al was bald, his translucent blue eyes vacant, his dyed goatee masking gray and his year round tan acquiring an unnatural orange hue after numerous visits to the stand up health club tanning bed. I can almost feel the slightly slick, oily sheen of his skin, bedewed by layers of baby oil, which he slathered on his skin in the blazing summer heat of his white plastic chair on the concrete of his restaurant parking lot. He worshiped the sun. He was an impressive 6'1, roughly two hundred and fifty pounds but very muscular and athletic. He lacked humility about his shapely legs, proudly boasting to us kids that his mother was related to Betty Grable, famed actress and singer from the 1940's, known for the best legs in Hollywood: *This is how we got our genetically muscular and shapely beautiful legs.*

The memories coil around me. Thinking back, thinking about Al, when Al was still Dad, reminds me of Mom.

Memories of her from my childhood taste like giant candy colored swirl lollipops on a long white stick. They smell like YSL Opium Perfume, which still lingers cloyingly around me, floating through the rooms and out the front door when she traveled down the hall from the bathroom, where she had applied staple crimson lipstick, had threaded heavy dangling gold earrings through her lobes, and had slipped on a pair of designer stilettos. I remember the clack of those heels as they confidently strutted the wood hallway floor before coming to a sudden stop, the shoes I loved so much that I'd run to her closet as soon as she left and would play dress up in them. At the front door, Mom paused, looked up at his face, and smiled humbly while he held up her treasured fur coat, which she easily slipped into. He whistled from the time he slapped on his Polo cologne until the moment they stepped into their golden carriage, a taxi cab. There was nothing sweeter to us kids than the pleasure of seeing them get ready for their night out on the town, an event smelling like joy and looking like love, a ritual continuing for years to come. I assumed they were happy; for many years, they were.

He was an only child with little support. He never shared his childhood memories with us but often alluded to raising himself with very little means. 'Role model' was a term that, in his childhood, was not only unheard of but also a bit preposterous: role models were for the weak. Al was a paradox. He was a fighter but hypersensitive; he was an entertainer but solitary; he was affectionate but devalued women. Perhaps these qualities had made him unpredictable and fearsome. I feared his nudity and his insatiable sexual appetite, the look in his disengaged, piercing blue eyes while he lounged on the green family room sofa naked underneath his open robe, completely exposed. Going through puberty was challenging enough without the image of my exposed father stretched out on the sofa. Al was strangely unsure about how to relate to or interact with me, almost as though I were a bizarre, foreign entity. Hindsight provides a certain degree of insight: he never understood the basic needs of an adolescent. He had raised himself, becoming a lone wolf, skulking, hiding behind a multitude of facades driven by desire and by instinct.

There was a shift in our family dynamics during this time, and I felt a palpable change, a crossing of boundaries more like a stomp than a tiptoe, occurring when I started becoming Al's friend instead of his daughter. It wasn't really a choice but more of a transition into a new role, starting when he began to slander my mother, who had begun to discover independence by returning to selling real estate. This new taste of freedom seemed a threat, and his insecurity and jealousy escalated so that he thrived off chaos, feeding off it daily, his perpetual fear that Mom was going to leave consuming him: he was almost willing it to happen. He'd unexpectedly lose control and behave erratically, threatening her life and, through osmosis, ours. Consequently, my relationship with him changed drastically.

Why did it change? The countless hours I spent trying to figure it out seemed purposeless. I vacillated between blaming him and blaming myself.

A father is a daughter's rock, her hero, her hope, her light, her strength. A rock chipped or split or broken is trying and hurtful. For me, the change in Al played a big part in my self-development. How he treated Mom, my siblings, and me, and others around us, family or not, affected me. Al was many things. He was happy, but he turned tragic; he was kind, but he turned vicious. Al and me biking, running, swimming and traveling when I was fifteen to St. Thomas, Virgin Islands without

Mom or siblings were happy adventures, loaded with laughter and with enjoyment of life to its fullest. But the moments of his uncontrollable anger and of my developing fear of him, and the moments of his total sorrow and of my paralyzed view of him, are memories dancing in my mind's eye. Mostly though, I remember always feeling connected to him.

Today, I don't fault him. He had a rough life full of abandonment. He was a boy from the West Town neighborhood of Chicago in the 60's when the area was considered ghetto. His mother had suffered from mental health issues and had abandoned him when he was young. The story has never been fully disclosed; sometimes I heard she moved to Michigan, and sometimes I heard she had died. Mom never met her. I craved details about my grandmother. I'm unsure whether Al blocked out the details due to an intolerable amount of pain and heartbreak or whether he was just simply ashamed of them.

Al lived with his paternal grandmother, whom he supported financially by working two jobs—shoe-shining and bussing tables. He never stopped caring for her. Later in life, he included her in Sunday brunches at the restaurant, where she sat stoically in her creaky wheelchair, observing. Great Grandma Emma was a no nonsense, white haired, strong willed German born feminist. She favored a severe, greasy ponytail and Coke bottle glasses usually held together at the sides with masking tape. She wore only beige, hand-knitted sweaters over printed dresses, both legs stuffed into nude nylons and thin-soled nursing shoes. She loved to eat sticks of butter.

Emma's son Leo, Al's father, had also left him at an impressionable age. The story told to me is that Leo bought *the joint,* where he tended bar. Then he realized he wanted out, and he planned to sell and to move to the suburbs. He reached out to Dad, at that time in his twenties; I was a year old. Dad claims he thought it was a dump and declined without a second thought, until he woke up a few months later in a cold sweat at the realization that he'd acted too quickly, without much thought. He'd made the wrong decision. By the time he had his epiphany and reached out to Leo, the joint had been purchased by somebody else. But *Al being Al* would find a way. He got in touch with the *somebody else* and persuaded him to sell it to him.

Both Leo and Al got their wish. Leo moved an hour out of town, perching himself on a hilltop, renting directly above another neighborhood bar. Al bought a business, began a new journey, and moved himself, Mom, and me to the apartment above the bar. Home sweet home.

Leo spent his days entombed in belongings, an authentic hoarder, living amid stacks of newspapers everywhere, cluttering both home and car. Where there was no newspaper were things wrapped in plastic baggies with thick, red rubber bands wrapped around them. Unlike his son, he lacked vanity, so much so that, when his beloved Irish Setter, Jake, knocked out his front teeth, he chose his homemade molded wax as a replacement for actual new teeth.

One day, Grandpa Leo announced that he had stopped drinking, cold turkey. He vowed to ride the train into the city every Sunday, which he did, year after year. He spent all Sundays on our couch reading the newspaper, napping, and collecting greenbacks from his son. He seemed to treasure those Sundays, bribing us with stacks of dollar bills, those same bills emanating from Dad, and with strange, teeth-staining, green mint leaf candies. Toward the end of his life, Al took him into his home and cared for him until he died. There was no wake or burial service or memorial service; I always regretted we were never given the chance to say goodbye . . .

Meeting Mom who was a waitress at the restaurant he managed made life make more sense for Dad, rounding out the jagged edges of family history and eliminating solitude. Mom was, for him, home at last. She was petite, childlike compared to his considerable frame. Her radiantly big bright blonde hair earned her a nickname from Dad, who called her *Fluff,* and her warm, deep blue eyes were gems captivating all those near her. She was an articulate Northwestern English major speaking softly with grace and intelligence. Her small town Indiana family projected perfection at church and in the community during a time when people internalized and hid their secrets. Al liked my grandparents' stability: they had been married fifty-seven years. Grandma was religious, never missing a church service and always singing in the choir, although Al was amused by her boxes of wine and cartons of cigarettes. Grandpa was genteel and generous, a cardiologist, and he pleased Al by patronizing Al's bar for cold beers and for watching Cubs games. Grandpa later thrilled us kids by building for us a heart-shaped pool (appropriately enough) in his Indiana backyard. Al's heart finally leaped for Mom's hand in marriage after falling in love with her immediately, head over heels. Mom was the angel there to save him; she was his dream come true, and her parents the idyllic fantasy family he had always wanted, later always gathering us together at Thanksgiving, Christmas, and for summer weekends to enjoy that pool and a pool house stocked with sodas, snacks, and popsicles, a grandchild's dream house always ready for inclement weather with the newest Nintendo and a trampoline in the basement.

Fluff was twenty-one when they married, and he was twenty-six. They stayed married for twenty years despite differing core beliefs and values. What's remarkable is that they made it work for as long as they did. Education, religion, finances, family, parenting, and health insurance, created conflict. In fact, every issue that mattered created conflict. Al was passive in the routine of family daily life unless pushed to extreme anger, and Mom was the active decision maker and rule enforcer. If not for my mother, a staunch believer in education, I believe that I would never have gone to college. She advocated its significance and wanted us to attend only the best schools. I'm still unsure whether Al finished high school; nonetheless, he instilled an ironclad work ethic, teaching us at a young age never to be dependent on anyone else financially or emotionally. We were taught to fend for ourselves.

Thus, my parents provided different perspectives and life experiences. Some made sense and worked; some did not. There were strengths and deficiencies in both approaches. One of the most baffling life choices, however, was my father's distrust in health insurance. He always cut corners. When my grandfather was dying in Dad's home, and he received past medical bills, he wrote DECEASED RETURN TO SENDER on the envelope before Grandpa had even passed. He assumed he was being ripped off and that doctors charged too much, anyway. He refused to be taken for an idiot and prided himself on self-perceived street smarts and in doing the opposite of what most people do in similar circumstances.

My maternal grandfather was a doctor for whom health insurance was essential, but Al considered monthly payments a waste of money. He felt that if anything catastrophic were to happen to any one of his five healthy children, he would take money out of the business to pay for it. That's what he believed in—taking cash from a metal box from under the bed. We had for decades the same pediatrician who gave us a family discount even when we were no longer children. They paid cash for the birth of all of their children, for our yearly check ups, for, stitches, and for my brother's recovery from being hit by a car, and for any other medical bill. I assumed this is what most, if not all, families did to pay up.

These differing views provided a gradual deterioration in my parents' relationship, and during my junior year of high school, a distinct change. The fighting seemed relentless. Al's drinking escalated, but Mom's drinking ceased, causing great conflict and resentment from Al. He believed, and aggressively voiced his view, that she was being unreasonable and irrational. His fury and explosive behavior became the norm, and he became a man to fear. Tiptoeing around him became a regular occurrence; walking normally, un-selfconsciously, with weightier, noisier steps, began uncommon.

Life with Dad became a bit like living in a spiraling tornado. Mom became withdrawn, suffering in silence. The only voices to be heard were those on the TV she seemed to live within while drinking coffee, one cup after another. I missed her. I missed them. I, too, succumbed to silence.

`The easy flow of money was eliminated, and Al stopped giving to us— period. I resorted to stealing cash from the infamous metal box under his bed to pay for clothes, activities, and meals. Whatever the need for money, I stole, until the rolling became a customary daily survival skill, a feeding frenzy of sorts. The contents of the box were there for the taking;

my sibs and I became street smart.

Every time the phone rang, I dug my nails into my sweating palms and held my breath until the continuous clanging stopped or the call was answered. Al abhorred the sound of the phone ringing, and there were times he'd forgotten to turn the ringer off. Those times I dreaded . . . *please stop ringing . . . please . . . just stop,* I whispered under my breath, jaws clenched.

Al told us the phone bill was too high and that he had set an empty Hills Brothers Coffee container next to the phone alongside a timer. If we wanted to call someone, we had a five minute time limit and were required to drop a few coins into that tin. This didn't last. Our apparent lack of follow through annoyed him to no end, and he simply ripped the cord out of the wall to disconnect our landline. It was strange and frightening knowing we could no longer reach the outside world by phone, my link to life outside the walls of sadness and of dysfunction. Fortunately, the pancake house across the street had a payphone, but my siblings and I felt utter desolation.

During a depressing episode in high school, I felt encroaching emotional exhaustion, the extra weight in my eyelids making it almost unbearable to open them fully, and I was thankful for weary eyes blocking unwanted sunlight like a raised shield. Light literally hurt. I remember lacking the strength to climb out of this black hole, as though I was covered by a cement blanket. Simply breathing sometimes exhausted me, so low the energy I could muster.

Therapy saved me. I finally started to feel heard and finally able to validate my feelings that the fighting between my parents was relentless and escalating to heights without a seeming ceiling, creating fear of the next explosion, occurring almost daily. Unloading to the therapist gave me the opportunity to claw my way out of that black hole of despair. The guilt I felt for leaving my siblings behind was constant, however, never quite leaving me, sort of like a shadow following me everywhere I went. But I needed to save myself. Attending a private college in Minnesota also seemed like the correct next step, a way to reset. College affirmed that my life had purpose, that I'd begin again.

I realized that returning home for Thanksgiving that first year was a bit of a gamble, like walking into an abyss. They had separated, and Mom had moved into a nearby apartment with my three youngest siblings. I hitched a ride home with a boy headed my way. I arrived at Mom's new digs to find it sparsely furnished and strewn with a few stray cats they had rescued along their way. But relief overtook worry. They were safe and could begin to live by setting those years of hell in the rear view mirror of memory. Mom was sober and sincere with drive and desire to create a new life for herself and her children. She moved valiantly forward, trying not to let the quicksand of the past suck her back in.

Al was devastated and became fully engaged in his own self-destruc-
tion, grieving all of us, but my sisters and I tried to preserve every bit of
Thanksgiving spirit, a forward march despite sadness weighing heavily
upon our holiday spirit. It was as though we were trying to stomp it out
with The traditional Turkey Trot run. After the race we stopped for a coffee at our usual spot while en route to see my grandparents, leaving Mom
and our youngest brother in the car. When we walked in, we saw Al at the
counter with a woman we had never seen before. Our initial excitement
overtook us, and we almost jogged over to him for a holiday hug. I stopped
short in mid stride when I saw him look over his shoulder and then shake
his hand away from his body, motioning us to leave without approaching
him. He feigned no knowledge of who we were. I stood beside the dessert
counter, yearning to reach out to him, needing his embrace but feeling
now as though I'd been punched in the stomach and the wind knocked
out of me. I stood there speechless, gasping until I could compose myself.
Al and the woman got their coffee and left.

I ran back to the car, head on my chest in shame, unable to comprehend
the chilly reception of my own father, whom I still loved. Tears streamed
down my face despite my desire to be strong for my sisters. I felt like a little
girl needing Mom to save me. Hold me, protect me. She was incapable of
that level of compassion or warmth, however, not a terrible thing, maybe,
but a sad fact. *Maybe he didn't see you* was all she managed to say.

We saw Al again a couple of days later and confronted him. His reply was precisely what I already expected and dreaded: *I can't let these women I'm dating know I have five children, or they will think I have baggage and won't want to date me anymore.* Baggage is part of the human experience, folks. We either have to own it or work through it, something he was incapable of doing. Consequently, we didn't speak for months, that is, I didn't speak to him for months. By the time I returned from spring break, he was on to another girlfriend.

Celia was from Costa Rica. She was twenty-three, and I was nineteen. She spoke not one word of English and also had a four year old daughter. Al had flown them in for an undetermined amount of time. I often wondered if the little girl might be his from years of his solo vacations. He called Mom's house and invited me over because he needed a translator so that they could communicate. Desperate for any connection with him, translator or daughter, it made no difference, I forged onward to Dad's one more time. I guess for that visit I wasn't baggage. She liked me, and I found myself liking her. She'd found a friend and confided in me about her struggles, expressing appreciation to Al for rescuing her. A familiar stab of jealousy pierced me momentarily—her knight, not mine. The next time I visited him, Celia and her daughter were gone. I asked Al what had happened but was answered with some vague explanation. I assumed he had tired of them and had sent them packing.

The more these 'Al episodes' occurred, the more independent I learned to become. Cash was a proponent in this journey; as Al said, *Cash is king*. He taught us to use only cash, to never accumulate debt. Thus, I used only cash. Financing college after my freshman year was no different, the same rules applying: cash only. I earned thousands of dollars bartending in Wrigleyville during Cubs season and at Al's bar throughout the school year. The stash funded both my full time undergraduate and graduate student education.

As my first year of college neared an end, my college experience was, without warning, suddenly wrested from me. It was time to register for my second year of classes, but there was a hold on my account because tuition hadn't been paid. When I called home to inquire, Al informed me that he would no longer be able to, or just didn't want to, pay for college due to the pending divorce. He said Fluff was taking him for everything, when, in fact, Mom settled for barely anything.

I remember the pit of my stomach freefalling, all the weight landing in my feet, now glued to the ground, which felt like it would plummet beneath me. Anger fueled hot tears. I wanted to say, *You fucking . . .* but I reassessed and reworked my thinking: *I wasn't that happy anyway; this college choice was a mistake.*

I had to come up with a plan quickly. I couldn't go back home, and so I decided impulsively to take a year off, and I moved to San Jose,

California. I rented a bedroom the size of a child's closet from a Japanese woman's home and volunteered as a corps member with City Year, an AmeriCorps affiliate for ten months of service work.

It was a transforming experience and gave me hope that I could accomplish anything at the ripe age of twenty. I returned to Chicago to go back to school and asked Dad if I could live with him in the gigantic, lonely, yellow Victorian home. I had direction, but it needed funding. I barely had enough to feed myself, any and all earned do-re-mi going straight to tuition. The deal was to work at Al's bar. The aphorism *The devil you know is better than the devil you don't know* had never rung truer.

I could breathe easier again, because I'd found my groove. Things were finally working again like a nicely oiled machine. Then came the call.

Butterflies flapped in my stomach like a full-fledged orchestra when I received out of the blue a call from an old fling. Apparently, he was planning on spending the summer in Wyoming and invited me to visit. I loved his sense of timing: I was obsessed with him, as I was with most guys. I was *boy crazy,* probably yearning for attention Al failed to provide, and surely searching for the affection and adoration I craved.

Wasting no time, I bought a ticket to visit him a week later, flying with my butterflies to Colorado, met there by a friend of his I didn't know who drove several hours to Wyoming. The setting was arrestingly beautiful, and in anticipation, my right foot pressed vicariously and impatiently down on the imaginary pedal. We finally arrived. I remember fondly the enthusiasm of the ceaseless partying into the night, the different voices, the laughter free of worry from the general weightiness of life. I liked this western mountain freedom, my latest escape.

I still hear the rocks under the tires of my mountain bike, random branches swooshing past and sometimes scratching my face as I flew down the trails, loving it, soaking in sunshine and the bowl of blue sky through the breaks in the trees, riding in my exhilaration much like daredevil Dad, cocky and arrogant on harrowing, steep, and narrow trails. I hit a branch hard at full speed and flipped like Dad Evel Knievel-like over handlebars vastly different from those Cheeto stained ones on my old Schwinn.

I heard only screaming from somewhere, from someone other than myself. But it was me. When I glanced down at my arm and saw that there was no longer a bone in my elbow and that it was dislocated down to my forearm, I screamed again. It took an hour to carry our bikes to the truck. The thirty minute drive on absurdly bumpy roads to the nearest hospital was sheer torture. The pain was unrelenting, excruciating, each bump on the road feeling like another break. When we arrived at the Emergency Room, they rolled me in immediately and assessed the break. I needed surgery and needed somebody to grant permission because I had no health insurance. The feeling of helplessness was indescribable. By the grace of God, someone called Al's bar in Chicago, and the bartender contacted my maternal grandparents. Grandpa paid for the ER visit and surgery. I needed a two week follow up, physical therapy, and a way home.

I had bought a one way ticket to Colorado because I had been planning to road trip back with everyone from Adventures of Wyoming. Al wouldn't fly me home, despite being able to afford it. A few days later, I road-tripped home with the old fling and several of his friends, humiliated by my weakness and by the need for additional hospital stops along the interstate because my hand kept turning blue. I felt useless, pathetic, and directionless.

A sense of shame can be crippling. It's like an octopus, shame forming the center and the tentacles representing all the different consequences shame grows. My entire being was being strangled by shame: I was penniless, homeless, jobless, disconsolate. I moved in with my new friend Kate whom I had befriended during my ten month stint in City Year. Her one bedroom apartment in Rogers Park was like a much needed drug, because it provided a sedative called solace. I took refuge in the isolation of her home, welcoming the shelter of walls and windows, the protection from the outside world which had, somehow, temporarily defeated me. I needed a place to fall apart and to rebuild. I guzzled coffee and smoked cigarettes on her porch while I contemplated life.

Jobless with an arm in a cast, I hatched a plan, not an exemplary plan but a path of action, nonetheless. Raspberry picking at my friend Christie's family farm in the suburbs. I could work with an empty milk carton around my neck and pick with my good hand, earning ten dollars hourly. I stayed with Christie's parents who also owned a wine distribution company, and were friendly with my parents. I took an online course, fulfilling a temporary need, but the time had come to pursue something a little more advanced.

I remember the fear while sitting in their kitchen to pick up the phone to call Al, pleading with him to let me come home yet again until I got my cast off. The relief was monumental when he agreed, welcoming me back. I returned to school in the fall and purchased insurance through the university, being without insurance no longer an option in my life! I attended school during the day and worked at the bar at night, earning a manager position the moment I turned twenty-one.

Making money helped rebuild my confidence, which provided courage to face Al strong and in control rather than needy and weak. Wonder Woman overnight I was not, but I was well on my way. Facing him head on with eye contact and without fear is the only way to handle a bully, which he was; maybe he was a pit bull. Our relationship slowly began to repair itself. My younger brother three years younger than I lived with us, which proved convenient. Exercise and music were both things we all had in common. We indulged in both pursuits, and we also treated ourselves to weed and booze, fueling partying back at the house. Al was a creature of habit, and this ritual became habitual.

Feeling connected to him was a little like walking on a tightrope over a cold, rocky river in a deep gorge. The rope was connected, and so it was walkable, yet at any moment a slip or a dangle or a plunge into unwelcoming water was not only possible but probable. Life at Al's had its perks, however. Wining and dining was high on the list. He had his favorites, the ritzy Shaw's Crab House downtown and an old Italian neighborhood joint, Sabatino's. Both venues felt like what decadence should feel like as we ordered hundreds of dollars worth of seafood and cocktails. It felt like nothing could go wrong while we sang lyrics to Frank Sinatra and Billy Joel songs at the piano, drinks in hand, living it up. After all, we were connected and Al always knew how to have a good time.

Alcohol made him vulnerable. He shared stories about his life, hardships, suffering, devastation, and loss due to the divorce. I saw the damage. Mostly, I felt special, proud, and high from happiness that he'd opened up to me, that he trusted me. And then I remember feeling utterly deflated and crushed, when, the next day, he never acknowledged any detail of our time together. Any hope that I had vanished in an instant. This pattern became intolerable, a rollercoaster that I could nolonger afford to ride. Thus, I left, moving out and in with friends in the Lakeview neighborhood. He and I remained in weekly contact about the bar, but it was all business until I graduated from college. Once I started my full time job as a social worker I was no longer useful to him.

We stopped talking.

I I I

BEE BABY

Dad taught me that rules don't apply. In some ways, this sensibility has served us both well. On the other hand, it offers a sense of grandiosity and of entitlement that has led to trouble on a path headed deep south. I choose to share my scars so others know they can heal, too. Because anyone experiencing life has scars. Is life doable? Can I make it through this day? The next? The one after? And if I do, will I achieve all I've ever dreamed of?

Sometimes a little help is needed, and that's where Bee-Baby came in. She was a woman who helped run our household above the tavern throughout my high school years, except for a brief hiatus when our family tried the suburb thing for a few years for some distance from the bar, but parents with five kids ran back to the city. The suburbs were too quiet. We didn't seem to fit in.

She was unforgettable: a three hundred pound African-American woman from the South Side of Chicago with many children from various partners. She favored wearing wifebeaters, the tighter the better, dark blue sweat pants with an elastic waist, and stark white keds that were always pristine. She loved nothing more than to talk to Al about her five pound weight losses. *Bee Baby you look good . . . lemme get a good look at you, Baby!* he'd say, jiving. Bee proudly did a little dance, twirling with a sassy finger snap for her reply, also complimenting herself in second person.

Bee Baby's nails were always long and painted bright, her hair was perfectly jheri-curled, and her bra was for one thing only— to stash her cash. Her chariot was a cobalt blue Dodge Spirit, fuzzy dice hanging from the mirror, a metal bat in the back for protection, just in case you failed to notice. We always awaited her arrival with bated breath: fearing highways, she chose side streets, lengthening her drive by an hour, at least. She took care of all the household chores—and she took care of us, prone to bury our faces in her ample bosom and to hug us like she meant it, which she did.

We knew her limits; we knew she meant it when she threatened to *whoop* us, and she was constant and much-needed. Bee Baby was like exotic distant family, and we were her *white grandbabies.* She was the ultimate storyteller. My best friend BK and I sat around the kitchen table while she entertained us with *hood* tales of violence and death. Proudly owning a gun she kept in her underwear drawer in case her ex-lover broke in, she reminded us how fortunate we were to feel safe.

When my parents' marriage crumbled, Bee Baby crumbled. One

morning, life with Bee came to a screeching halt. I remember waiting by the window anticipating her arrival to discuss the new family dynamics. She seemed to really "get" me. I waited for her *Foxy Lady* Dodge Spirit, for that glint of blue rolling my way. It never came, and she never came back. Al must have told her to stop coming. There came no call, no good-bye, no nothing. An instantaneous flow of hostility charged forward from within me, downright furious foot stomping: *How could Al take another positive thing away from us? As a lost seventeen year old, I needed her more than ever.* Tears flowed. We never got to say goodbye, and I missed her in ways that still hurt. I longed for her warmth, the way she made me laugh, and her pure love. Bee Baby, my Foxy Lady, oh how I miss you.

I V

HANDYMAN

Bee never left my heart. She was no longer here anymore to protect me or to handle things, things such as him. So I held her memory near and dear, like a secret saint guiding me during that three year hiatus in the suburbs. He seemed not so awful at first, not really. He was short and skinny with slick skin covered by a few unimpressive homemade tats, his mousy, stringy hair mostly hidden by a paint-stained navy blue bandana. His flannel shirt had ripped off sleeves to show what he thought were muscles, which he flexed subtly; he also proudly flashed yellow work boots.

He resembled Popeye! He was amusing and harmless, like another distant member of the family, another Al stray who could fix things. I remember that fourth grade move into the big house, the money pit. It needed a lot of work and a handyman. Al wasn't the handy type, but he was resourceful. He hired the handyman.

I remember the excitement of wandering through a new domain, touching each wall in each new room, smelling the plaster on the walls, peeling the corners of some of the old wallpaper in the bathroom, and jumping up and down on any wood, uncarpeted floors to see what creaked and what didn't. Each window pane was cool and musty with dust when I pressed my face to the glass.

The handyman worked on various projects throughout the day and then lingered, entertaining Al throughout the evening. He strummed the guitar while we roasted marshmallows. I could smell the beer on Al's breath when he laughed and sang. I still see the handyman's face, the overly friendly smile seeming not quite genuine.

His daughter was my age, and we became friends. She eagerly pursued our friendship, wanting a sleepover buddy, seeming desperate for company, as though she needed an ally. Reflecting on that first day, there's one thing in particular that stood out. The handyman and his daughter and I piled into his banana yellow, windowless van bereft of back seats. We shoved the tools to the back for floor space during a ride somewhere. Unease washed over me like a mammoth wave when we jumped out of the van onto a path. I looked ahead and espied a dilapidated shack nestled in woods amid overgrown grass, reminding me of the house in Hansel and Gretel.

The house and the trees did not frighten me, but the darkness did, presenting a palpable warning subsiding slightly with the invitation to watch R rated movies. I sat cross-legged, Indian style, between the handyman and his daughter on a dirty and stained, carpeted floor. His wife, rail-thin and unwashed, with bulging brown eyes, appeared briefly before retreating back into a bedroom, where she stayed. That night, my first visit there, he requested we girls take a bath before bed because we had been outside playing all day. At the time, I didn't think it was strange that the handyman would bathe his daughter and me or wash our hair. I actually thought it was super nice that her father paid so much attention to us. He seemed like such a cool dad, so involved. I thought maybe this special attention was a perk of the Only Child.

After the bath—the smell of Pert Plus still causes nausea—we stepped into our PJs, ate the warm, buttery popcorn he served, and hopped into the creaky, loose-spring, pull-out bed transformed from the ragged sofa. Suddenly, he climbed in, too, placing himself between his daughter and me. She fell asleep before me, most likely so quickly because, that night, she felt she could sleep safely.

When it was time to turn out the lights, he snuggled up close behind me, spooning me sickeningly while rubbing my legs. Then he scissor-kicked my legs between his and with his hands on my hips, fingers digging into them, crawling their way downward, he moved my hips back and forth, teaching me how to dry hump without ever saying a word to me. I felt his hard penis in his white long underwear poking my back, his heart pounding, his breathing labored and deep. My heart thumped like thunder, and I gasped for air in terror and confusion. The warmth developing down there felt good, but I knew it shouldn't. I shut my eyes tight and prayed that he would just leave me alone. He didn't, and I didn't want to feel like a bad girl. I felt sick. I pretended to fall asleep, praying . . . .Everything hurt, and everything felt wrong. I opened my eyes to stare at my sleeping friend, not daring to move, while he continued to dry hump my behind. Finally, he groaned loudly, and it ended. I didn't move. I kept silent. I froze like a statue and hardly breathed until he quietly crept out of bed and tiptoed like a child into his bedroom to join his wife.

Morning brought shame. He'd gone out for donuts and had returned to make pancakes, carrying on as though nothing had happened, and I played along, knowing at my young age no other way to cope. For several weeks, he returned to our house, to fix things and to play Sleeping Beauty in the basement. I wasn't allowed to wake up until our prince kissed us. Then, just like that, he'd go back to fixing the back porch.

One Monday after a weekend rendezvous with the Handyman, I was in class learning about the Catholic version of Family Life—basically, sex or, preferably, abstinence. The teacher covered inappropriate versus appropriate touch, and I felt like the worst ten year old ever. I'd committed a mortal sin. There was no doubt that I was going to hell unless I confessed to God. I went home from school that day terrified but strengthened by the correctness of my mission, and asked Dad if I could speak to him privately in my room. I'm unsure why I told him instead of Mom, maybe because Dad was big and robust, and I wanted him to protect me. Maybe Mom seemed more overwhelmed by day to day parenting, something I can relate to now that I'm a mom.

He stood at my window, arms crossed in front of his chest, glancing outside as though this chat would likely waste his time. He leaned on the desk, hand right next to my record player as my favorite Bangles song Manic Monday played softly. I told him what had been happening, and he didn't believe me. He said if it was really happening, then why did I continue to go to their house? Why hadn't I spoken up sooner? My interpretation was, This is your fault.

Then Al switched gears by declaring that he would kill the handyman if my story was, in fact, true. Stupefied, I felt conflicted about whether I wanted Dad to rescue and avenge me or to spare the handyman's life. What had I done? I wanted to take it all back. I wished I'd never said anything. I begged him to just forget about it. I vowed never to return to his house. He continued to be our handyman, and I avoided him.

Strangely, I continued to experience random, dirty men flashing me their penises, and I began to wonder whether I was attracting this attention, like an unadulterated magnet for all things perverse. I recall waiting at the city bus stop on my way home from high school on days I had to take the bus. I seemed to sense that something might happen, maybe because I emitted a certain energy or a non-human sound wave only deviants heard, one saying Hey you! Flash me! Lo and behold, a man in a white pickup truck pulled up to the curb, stroking his penis and licking his lips, beckoning until the light changed, for me to come over to him. I looked quickly away and waved to a group of people so it looked as though I weren't alone.

This fright occurred multiple times during my four years of high school. I learned the art of concealing, always carrying in my backpack a baggy, unassuming set of clothes to change into before I left for the bus, preventing enticing anyone by my pleated uniform skirt. I hid my blonde hair under my winter hat because I feared anyone finding me attractive. I kept my guard up by continuing well into my teens full sniper fashion camouflage when traveling.

When I was sixteen and at the height of my eating disorder at the beginning of the unraveling of my parents' marriage, rage-laden and hysterical, I confronted Dad about disbelieving me about the handyman. I wanted and needed him to acknowledge his mistake and to apologize for not protecting me. He wrapped his arms around me and held me tightly while I sobbed in his arms. He said nothing.

V

E D

I focused all my energy on staying as busy as possible when my parents' marriage started falling apart. I had an eating disorder, which was getting the better of me. Similar to addictions such as alcoholism, sex, and gambling, there is a progression in developing an eating disorder. When I was nine, I could hardly wait to start my hip hop dance class in order to see myself in a black leotard. Ashamed of my reflection in the giant wall of unyielding mirrors saying, *You're so fat,* I compared my distended stomach to the other girls in class. I had to resist the urge to run out of the studio and put my sweatsuit back on. This is my first memory of comparing myself to other girls and of not feeling *good enough,* although I was by no means a chubby kid.

I sat at the kitchen counter with my twelve year old legs stretched against the wall and called Mom over because I thought my knees looked fat. I thought there was something wrong with me. I believed my body defective, disfigured, and needing to hide itself. Did my body perception differ from the observation of others? When we moved from the suburbs back to the city, we moved farther west of the bar to a neighborhood called Old Irving Park and lived next door to a YMCA. I took my siblings to open gym to play basketball while I attended step aerobics class religiously on weekends, twice per day. As an eighth grader, I was the youngest person in the class, but I felt strong and extremely capable. Mom took the classes with me. In addition to staying skinny and feeling more in control, she and I enjoyed a special bonding time without Dad and my brothers and sisters.

I was also nourishing my irrational strive for perfection. Rising from the kitchen table at any given meal to trudge to the fridge was a gamble. *A moment on your lips is a life time on your hips.* This was Al's most cherished mealtime phrase reminding us not to overeat, which finally triggered hiding *when* I ate and *what* I ate. I stuffed food under my shirt, up my sleeves, and in my backpack. In full stealth mode, I snuck into my bedroom to binge, traveling from one food group to another: sweets, tasty, carbs—maybe repeating carbs—in my food free-for-all, which ended only when I decided I should lock myself in the bathroom for thirty minutes to let the faucet fill the tub to drown out the noise of my purge to feather-light emptiness. I lied to myself like a sociopath, promising that I would never do it again, only to repeat the process a few hours later, or hating myself so intensely, I ate nothing for several days.

Al encouraged us to engage in an active lifestyle: *Make sure to exercise but not on a bike—that's for lazy people; you'll get fat secretary ass.* I'm more intensely motivated when people tell me I can't or shouldn't do something, and so I rode my bike twenty-two miles round trip from Chicago to high school on the North Shore, mostly out of the saddle. I became a spin instructor years later. Riding a bike has been a therapeutic tool for me. I make a playlist, crank it up loudly, and get lost for a while. Forget you can't . . . because you can. As I turn up the tension on the bike, I push harder and say the words *Get it, Girl,* truly believing in myself that I can do anything and always feeling inspired when I finish.

My eating disorder was, in my opinion, predictable and safe. I was in total control of my coping mechanism, or so I thought. Bulimarexia (not specifically a DSM V diagnosis, classified as Eating Disorder NOS because it doesn't specifically meet criteria for Anorexia or Bulimia) allowed me to mask the uncomfortable feelings I had no clue about how to process. The act of restricting felt like a necessary punishment. My internal dialogue went something like *Somebody please look at how badly I'm hurting; when I use my words, nobody seems to hear me.* Maybe someone would hear my audible words or, rather, my body language—the log in a food and exercise journal, the diet pills, laxatives, enemas, and the bottles of water to induce vomiting.

I did the family grocery shopping once a week with hundreds of dollars to buy whatever I wanted, probably a bad idea for someone struggling with an eating disorder. Every aisle was a hazard zone. I would over-exercise at the gym and return home with fresh resolve, but I found it impossible to focus on homework or TV and instead resumed my unceasing exercising, sets of lunges, fire-hydrant leg lifts, and Jane Fonda sit-ups after dinner—*if* I ate dinner. Although my parents were restaurateurs, nobody particularly liked to cook. Al occasionally grilled or ordered in, Bee concocted the most cheese and butter loaded mac and cheese ever, or we snacked all evening.

I had to be constantly moving—always, the definition of insanity. I wanted to feel more pain, pleading for it, just to feel and to fill myself with activity in order to end the emotional emptiness, the gaping emotional hole. I identified with the song *She Talks to Angels,* released in 1989 by the Black Crowes, and played it repeatedly. *She never mentions the word addiction in certain company. Pain gonna make everything alright. Says she talk to angels.*

I endured this exhausting cycle perpetually, bingeing, purging, exercising, restricting, repeating, permitting thoughts and rituals related only to food and body image. I was never satisfied, however, never able to fill the void by achieving the dream, the fantasy of reaching the goal of *liking myself* by maintaining a weight of exactly one hundred pounds, not one pound over or under. I allowed a number to give me value. Loving myself was never within the realm of possibility; the best I could hope for was *to like.*

It takes one to know one was apt. I spotted a few high school friends I believed also suffered from eating disorders. I tactfully inquired, and we did, indeed, share a secret. We tried to support one another in our common goal to get healthy, but it backfired when we became competitive, escalating our disorder.

Life became a stresser. I felt anxiety in the most trivial, conventional scenarios, such as dinner. I was kindly invited to Sunday dinners at my high school boyfriend's home, his family aware that my parents' marriage was on the rocks, and I appreciated their traditional, seemingly intact family dynamics and the escape from my own family, but the ritual became an anxiety provoking event. I wanted no attention while I ate, which had become a private activity. I always wondered if they thought I consumed too much or too little. When I did allow myself to eat, I was unable to stop until I had become bloated, in pain and full to the point of needing to eliminate. After dinner, I excused myself for a run to the bathroom and purged, but during one episode I clogged the toilet. I panicked. Someone was going to find out. I was mortified. First, I needed to fix the plumbing, and then I needed to figure out how I was going to evacuate the rest of the food because of intense discomfort. Both endeavors seemed equally imperative, but all I wanted to do was to escape this tiny, dark bathroom of hideous wallpaper and get the hell out of there. I concocted an excuse, which I'd become quite good at, claiming to have lost track of time when I had homework to finish.

I ran to my car and tore out of their driveway, my mind on the nearest 7-Eleven. I careened into the first gas station and bought a large bag of Doritos, a bottled water, a Diet Coke, and a pack of Parliament Lights. I wolfed down the Doritos, shoveling in several chips at a time, chugged the water, and threw up everything into the plastic bag while still driving. When I was through, I popped open the Diet Coke, lit a cigarette, and pressed play on the cassette player. The Dave Matthews Band always soothed me.

I am unsure whether my parents noticed my progressive deterioration; frankly, I am sure they were never oblivious, but nothing was . said. My best friend BK noticed: I dropped out of track, never ordered food when we went out, and was always distressed about eating with her because, once I started, I feared losing control. I sat alone at lunch and often visited the library instead, avoiding food altogether unless alone. BK accused me of being moody and irritable and eventually confronted me about the food problem, told a teacher, and my mother. I despised her for it and envied her petite frame and ability to eat anything she wanted without consequence. She seemed so utterly at ease with her body, so comfortable in her own skin. Her wardrobe was one to envy, and I had loved to borrow her clothes but could never suck my gut in tight enough to pull her jeans on over my *Baby got back*. She was unable to fathom my hell. None of this was her concern, anyway; why did she want to meddle, possibly ruin my life? Her busybody invasion threatened my desire to live, my very existence!

I chose to live.

Finally, I was able to summon the courage to stop denying I had a problem, and I surrendered. Mom was there to support me and researched until she located an eating disorder specialist, surprising me. Because Fluff was petite and beautiful, like BK, I had presumed she would be unable to understand my challenge. In my eyes, she was perfect; how could she possibly comprehend or tolerate imperfection? Thus, I had never confided in her. Able at last to voice my pain and distress, I still feared her reaction, but she had "heard" and would help me heal. I was no longer alone.

The next day, I saw a nutritionist for meal planning. Becky was maternal in spirit and hip in style. She had spiked white hair and wore multiple beaded bracelets running up her arms. She wore a tank top and fitted Capri pants with a belt wrapped around her tiny waist, her figure inspiring, toned, and *healthy*. She sipped tea quietly and methodically while I divulged my fears of food. Becky taught me a better relationship with meals by proceeding with a *good food/bad food* list, her goal foods I could tolerate and keep down. She taught me healthy fats, proteins, and mindful eating. She became my savior.

There was something more frightening about the purely medical aspect of my treatment, however, which seemed sterile, cold, and clinically void of nurture. I needed bone density testing and an electrolytes analysis out of concern I'd seriously damaged myself. A psychiatrist prescribed Prozac to ease anxiety and to curb impulses. This team of providers helped me immensely. I am eternally grateful.

All the professional opinions recommended family therapy, but there was one major problem with their suggestion: Al was unaware of my eating disorder, unless he was feigning ignorance of it. He also had no idea that I was in treatment, but Fluff took the recommendation to heart and insisted to Dad that the entire family needed a family session, because *I was struggling*. Characteristically, he never said a word.

A week later, everyone piled into Mom's red Jeep Cherokee for the trip to our first family session, reminiscent of the family forays to Sabatino's in happier days. Now, there was complete silence and no Sabatino's with a ubiquitous maitre d', no bartender with a shaker rattling like a castanet. The tension in the waiting room was palpable, so taut I feared I might snap. Our glum silence continued, punctuated only by the ringing phone and the responding receptionist. I welcomed eavesdropping on her conversations to relieve the tedium of avoiding eye contact with my family, studying instead the fibers in the gray carpet beneath our nervously tapping feet. My heart pounded resoundingly in my ears and in the back of my throat, and I considered fleeing. Still contemplating my options, an elegant Asian lady in a beautiful suit greeted us, introducing herself as Amy, the family therapist, and asked us to follow her to her office. She began by gathering information and by reviewing protocol, and the tension evaporated until Al suddenly lost it, shooting upright and yelling, completely out of control: *All you therapists do is create problems for people . . . We were doing just fine until you came along . . . Doesn't everyone have body issues? . . . Why the hell are you making such a big deal about this?* . . . Amy's face turned red, and she fumbled for words while the rest of us sat frozen in the silence of embarrassment until Al angrily rounded us up, and we exited en masse. This was all my fault. I wanted to apologize to Amy for Al's behavior and to my family for creating problems, for which the only solution was continuing what I'd started. Thus, I empowered myself to pursue individual treatment without my family. I needed to get better for *my sake.* I would do it *myself.* Serendipitously, the experience persuaded me to become a social worker and a champion for others who can't champion themselves.

I faithfully practiced the self-help effort until I left for college in 1996. Mom and Dad drove me to the school, and nails on the chalkboard is the most accurate analogy for that six hour drive. I clenched my jaws and forced myself to control breathing impatient with anticipation, and Al seemed impatient to arrive, too. The day brightened only upon reaching our destination. The routine of settling in ensued with awkward intervals of muttering and of useless banter, a few hugs and tears from me before they were gone, and, suddenly, I was alone. *Suck it up,* Kelley, I told myself. I was now free and eager to get back on track, racing against my demons lest they catch up. Fear taunted me throughout the day, mostly around meal time. I feared a potential relapse, yet I was determined to be *my* ideal student, well-rounded and able to cope. At last, there were no barriers. I tried it all—guitar, crew team, party, run, party, volunteering—in pursuit of my groove, my thing. Nothing fit, however, and that familiar desolation began to sneak up on me. Most people hung out in groups, but I was always much better one on one. Still prone to a bit of social anxiety, drinking helped take the edge off.

My younger sister called each week pleading with me to come home. Things had escalated. According to my siblings, 'home' had gotten really bad. I knew I would never leave school, but I desperately wanted refuge for my sister, who had taken over my caretaker role. The next weekend, she flew out to Minnesota alone, a thirteen year old, confused girl seeking respite, and she partied with me, both of us roaming together like a couple of stray cats, angry, sad, confused, consistently scared, and, finally, exhausted.

Subsequent to my little sister's visit was a visit by Mom herself for a campus Bodeans concert with me. I tried to glean all the information I could about what had happened at home. We stayed up late, and she hung out at the bar with my friends and me, although she no longer drank. Cigarette in hand, Fluff owned the pool table and beat with a cool smile every man daring to challenge her. That was MY mom, cool, strong, beautiful, new and improved.

I was proud of Mom's valiance ignoring others' commentary or advice to stay with Al for the kids sake. I'm a product of divorce and a trained therapist. I don't support this mentality. A marital relationship is the first relationship experience our children observe. If there's yelling, swearing, and physical or emotional abuse, children come to believe this is a normal way to treat someone you are in a relationship with. Surely, if both parties are open, able, and willing to work through a difficult marriage, that's a different story. There are plenty of couples I've treated over the years who have decided to divorce amicably, and we talk about healthy ways to co-parent and to break the news to the kids. Divorce doesn't have to be knock-down, drag-out ugly. Make sure the top priority is in the best interest of the children, facilitated by open lines of communication within the family unit. We never sat down together to discuss what was going on within the family, creating a lot of anxiety and uncertainty. My siblings and I were left to observe the decline of the marriage and to make our own assumptions.

My relationship with Dad continued to be tumultuous. He was unable to control himself, always commenting on the way I looked. Had I lost weight? How much money was I making? He measured my value through external accomplishments. Naturally, this is how I appraised my own value for years to come, but, fortunately and gradually, body image became no part of the equation. I had been knocked down but had found a way to rise again.

V I

B K

I think often of eighth grade, the last year of elementary school, and I was the new kid at a new school. I was a scrappy basketball player, full of energy, full of life, and aggressive. *Balls to the wall.* I spent more time on the court floor wrestling with an opponent than on my feet running down the court. I wanted to fight. One of those opponents became my rival, short, blonde, and mouthy, a firecracker fully loaded. She was my nemesis, and I was hers. A year later, I was apparently the only person from my grade school to attend the all girls high school of Mom's choice. I didn't know a soul. I walked into the colossal high school auditorium, scanning the huge, echoing space and pacing my breathing while I got my schoolbooks for the year, and I spotted my old rival at a distance. There was a momentary assessment before reciprocal introductions. From that moment on, we were best friends, both of us from alcoholic families, which assured instant bonding. We grew close fast, our interests—boys, drinking, and sports—sealing the deal. We spent hours on my bedroom window ledge listening to Led Zeppelin, *Stairway to Heaven,* smoking one cigarette after another like two serious *bad asses.* We cherished risk taking and needed it after befriending a group of older boys who were taggers, part of a gang, lending them a roughness making them even more seductive to two blonde Catholic girls enjoying feeling like renegades after hanging out, unaccounted for, with the taggers in neighborhood alleys drinking Mad Dog out of paper bags. Hours blurred into days, and bowling alleys became dive bars before and after Grateful Dead concerts.

On the other hand, I loved campus ministry, musical theatre, travel, volunteering, and leading retreats. I thrived on climbing the social ladder, attending upperclassmen parties, dating my new, long term boyfriend, and sneaking out for midnight joy rides in Al's fully loaded BMW. BK worked at the Mercantile Exchange during the summer before our senior year. I remember the thrill of getting ready for a night out in the posh part of town called the Viagra Triangle, always obsessing over which outfit to wear. I still feel the humidity and the subtle breeze valiantly trying to waft through my bedroom window while I applied pink, frosted lip gloss, my pupils adjusting to the shifting, dimming light of gloaming, my body energized with mounting anticipation of our rendezvous with older men, whom we joined for Happy Hour on Fridays after work. They did what older men customarily did, paying for our drinks and treating us with respect, although we knew we had no business being there. We felt too special and sophisticated and safe here, however, to stay away from this stark contrast to back alley bars, this sleek alternative to furtive paper bags.

I was conflicted about who or what I really wanted to be. Eventually, it came time for BK and me. We attended different colleges, but I frequently visited her in Dayton, Ohio, where we continued binge drinking and hanging out with as many boys as possible. In our junior year, we traveled to Europe to study abroad, she to Ireland and I to Spain. Although I visited her, I recall little, sadly, mostly a haze, like living within a blizzard, a fast, exciting, blurry, and opaque memory diffused by one discoteca to the next, one pitcher of Red Bull and vodka after another.

When we graduated, we decided on graduate school in Chicago and shared an apartment with another of our best friends, Susan. *The Three Musketeers* we became! We talked, laughed, dreamed, and partied. We shared career hopes and dreams of marriages and children. We fantasized about living the fairy tale. I worked hard toward that goal, that imaginary wonderful life always in my mind's eye, and that life, which a few years back had seemed unattainable, began to come true. I'd like to be able to say *Once upon a time,* but it was never quite like that. That life began for me when I got engaged and moved to Santa Monica. BK visited, and we hiked, talked, laughed, and dreamed like always.

We enjoyed a trip to an authentic Mexican restaurant or to a club or two on Hollywood Boulevard. No catastrophes occurred, thus far, and my new found fairy tale life remained intact. One of those weekends together, we decided to meet in Vegas, and I had been *dry* for a few months without telling her. At the time, I was unsure why I had never told her; perhaps I was afraid she would cancel, not wanting to see me. Divulging did create a strain on our time together: drinking had played a major role in our relationship, and it played a major role in Vegas, too, but we got through it.

When my husband, three children, and I moved back to Chicago after six years in Santa Monica, BK and I picked up right where we had left off, again becoming *the dynamic duo.* We've fought like sisters, shared joys, tears, milestones, travel, running adventures and deep heartaches. She remains my best friend to this day.

V I I

H P

The word *friend* seems so glibly tossed about the past decade, as though any random encounter produces an instant pal. Social media *friends* seem to replace nowadays a *real* relationship, and hip reaction emotions and reactions supplant real live feelings, emotions and reactions. Cyberspace friends don't yet know the real you, creating a challenge for them to truly support and guide you. I'm not diminishing the power of social media; I am true fan, but I am also an advocate of all things *REAL*. Therefore, I try to be as genuine as possible in my social media *Shares* even if they may never get the popular vote. I've enjoyed dozens of deep, face-to- face coffee dates prompted by social media reconnections, which have enhanced my life because we meet and take our masks off, meeting and getting to know our authentic selves by sharing in real time.

I'm eternally grateful for those close to me, such as my dear friend Susan. She introduced me to *The Power of Now,* by Eckhart Tolle, around the time we were both embarking upon motherhood. She suggested the book because we had discussed our long lists of future goals, both wanting to anticipate them without worry, anxiety, or an overbearing sense of *I can't do this*. Eckhart is a contemporary spiritual healer unaligned with any particular religion or tradition, describing experiences as being neither positive or negative, and stating in a nonjudgmental voice, *The only sane way to live is by accepting what is*. I try my best to live according to this philosophy rather than by adhering to any religious tenets.

I was baptized Lutheran but attended twelve years of Catholic school, which had been chosen for overall education and situational convenience rather than for religious inculcation. Growing up in an urban environment in the early 80's, public school never seemed a valid option, regardless of its convenience. Mornings were chaotic in our household: different schools, different schedules. Al hired Florentino, a fiftyish man from El Salvador who doubled as the clean up guy at Al's bar, to drive me to high school. He was gentle, patient, lovely, and kind. He was always immaculately clean cut and crisp, his hair perfectly parted and neatly combed. His version of a standard uniform was a pair of ironed jeans with a crease, a dark T-shirt, and a London Fog navy blue jacket. He picked me up in his spotless, silver, two door Honda promptly at seven A.M., always popping out of the car to open the passenger door for me. En route, we played a homemade version of ESL. Florentino barely spoke English, and my Spanish was equally rudimentary. We coped by tuning in to Spanish radio, while I tried to question him in Spanish, and he tried to answer in English. I am sure neither one of us knew what the other was saying!

Most students at my North Shore high school drove Jeep Cherokees or were dropped off in their parents' Jaguars, Mercedes, or BMW's, and I was embarrassed arriving at the front entrance in a jalopy with someone apparently not my parent. I politely asked him not to open the door for me, and I'm embarrased now, today, remembering that reaction. Fortunately, Al chided that I was privileged and blessed to have *a driver.* I can hear him now, saying in his distinctive Chicago accent, *Hey, Kel, what's better den dat?*

While I clambered from the car, Florentino said, every day, *Bye, Miss Kelley. Have good day. I see you tomorrow.* His pride in and gratitude for the life he enjoyed was heartwarming and contagious. Mom called these special encounters with others *God Winks,* referring to something *working out after all,* serendipitously, and spiritually. I was indeed relieved that I never had to take the bus and realized I was beholden to Florentino—I was also relieved when I got my license and could drive Mom's old Jeep Cherokee.

Growing up in Chicago was a front row seat to a multicultural runway. I was exposed to many cultures divided exclusively by neighborhoods. The Italians lived in the Italian neighborhood, the Greeks in the Greek neighborhood, the Polish in the Polish neighborhood, and so forth. I observed different cultures but never participated in their traditions, as though the whole world spun inside a colossal translucent bubble I merely observed outside it.

I never knew my nationality, causing confusion at times. We were told there was a combination of Swedish, Dutch, and Norwegian from my mother, and German from Al. Al turned flip by telling us we could be whatever we wanted. Nobody would know the difference. Thus, I didn't know who I was, and I was unsure what I wanted to be. One of my brothers chose to be Italian, wearing gold chains around his neck, black Z Cavariccis, his hair slicked back with gel. My other brother chose to be African-American, donning Nike from head to toe, his shorts hanging just below his buttocks, and dating black girls only, wooing them by sporting real diamond studded earrings and by speaking slang. Serendipitously, his choice carried some weight: he got a full ride to play college basketball with his best friend, Michael Jordan's son.

I ended up marrying Irish and surrounded by Catholicism most of my life. Maybe I was meant to be Irish and just never realized it at the time. Perhaps the ethnic choice was made for me. The journey of spirituality is longlasting, loaded with ebbs and flows, and it may be stronger or weaker at different points in our life. Sometimes we are called to God, or we search for God when life gets tricky or overwhelming, even if God isn't part of our daily life. Why does our bond with God become stronger when we prepare for death or face a life or death situation or deal with trauma or battle a financial crisis? Why do we choose to wait so long?

I realized a common thread throughout most of my adventures and experiences—overindulgence, perpetually bingeing, always wanting everything, more money, more food, more clothes, more booze, more toys, more, more, more! Al desired more of everything, too. We both craved more, better. Nothing seemed to be enough.

Florentino, happy and easily satisfied, always intrigued me: what had he risked to come to America? Who had he left behind? What had he endured? Did he have children he'd never see again? How many days did he go without food, water, or shelter? Somehow, his appreciation and gratitude for the little, inalienable things was an unequivocal, monumental example to others.

Often, I remember ghetto blasters and wall phones fulfilling our basic needs. There was no email, no text, less immediate gratification. Some people found joy in the anticipation of improvements. Today, we become impatient if someone fails to respond to us immediately. I'm at the top of the list, but I crave simplicity. Most of the people emigrating to the United States do so in hope of a better life. I needed to remove myself from the United States and live in Central or South America. I needed to start over.

SPIRITUAL ADVENTURE NUMBER ONE

In January of my freshman year in college, I had the opportunity to entrench myself in volunteer work in San Lucas Toliman, Guatemala. Eleven other students and I helped build a medical clinic and worked in coffee fields. The most gratifying experience, however, was being part of a unique solidarity, a unity with the villagers. The memory of those children is indelible. We played with them for countless hours outdoors in unrelenting heat. They were filthy, legs and feet caked in mud and covered with cuts, hair mangled, overgrown, and infested with lice. Yet their smiles were immense and genuine. Surely they were the happiest children I had ever seen.

They had nothing. We provided them with toothbrushes and paste and taught them the importance of oral hygiene, something most of us Americans probably take for granted. They were unconcerned with superficial things; what they wanted most was genuine human contact. I had the good fortune of joining forces with some of the doctors there for the sole purpose of performing cleft palate surgery. Upon arrival at the clinic, we were greeted by a sea of pleading parents who had waited for hours, all hoping and praying that their child would receive this free of charge procedure. To say they appreciated the opportunity is a gross understatement; their gratitude was third-world unworldly.

After the cleft palate operations, we visited a local orphanage. Laughter, screeches of triumphant, pure joy echoed throughout the place. We read to them donated story books and played on dirt floors the few games they presented to us. I stared at the earth, realizing it represented comfort and safety and beds to these children. I flashed back to that brown carpet in my childhood, shaggy but soft and warm and littered with a pile of toys from my huge toy chest. The kids stretched out in rows on their bedbug-infested mattresses, as though they lay on high thread count linens and pillows in a bed fit for a queen, and I appreciated the memory of my warm, fluffy Ralph Lauren bed; I thought about Dad, tightly wrapping me in firmly tucked sheets. The kids attached themselves to us with joyous, spirited love each night, and when we parted, kissed us and said, *Duerme con los angelitos.* Tears blurred my eyes when I waved goodbye: *they* were the angels.

I realized I needed to *give more.* After my freshman year, I decided to take a gap year and became a member of City Year San Jose. There are over nineteen thousand corps members in twenty-five cities throughout the U.S. I worked with a corps of fifty, ages seventeen through twenty-four, ranging from high school dropouts to college graduates. I was on a team of ten with a wide range in ethnicity, intelligence, socioeconomics, and religion. The job was an ideal but challenging opportunity. Here, I met Kate. She was from the Midwest, a graduate of Northwestern, who, by absolute coincidence, frequently ate at one of my family's restaurants close to campus where my parents met. We were roughly the same age with similar physical characteristics. We are naturally drawn to people who look like ourselves or with whom we share similar life experiences, and this was true of Kate and me and our double portion.

SPIRITUAL ADVENTURE NUMBER TWO

The skills I learned at City Year proved invaluable. I worked at inner city schools as an ESL (English as a second language) assistant, helping to create after school programs. As a Team Liaison, my job was to collaborate with significant corporate sponsors in the hope of encouraging volunteering and sponsorship. After ten months of community service, I earned a $4,725 scholarship form AmeriCorps, a program Bill Clinton had initiated. I realized I wanted to return to Chicago, to become fluent in Spanish, and to study social work at The University of Illinois.

The opportunity to study abroad in Seville, Spain presented itself after my first semester home, and I jumped headlong into another adventure, a transition into a completely different culture, and I was wildly excited about fully immersing into this new life. The plan was for me to live with an older Spanish woman, Pilar, and her daughter in a two-bedroom apartment. I would room with Christie. Her family owned the raspberry farm where I had worked with one arm in cast. How much had happened since then?

Here we were years later, together again in a foreign country, almost like reaching for the stars. Stars are quite distant, and so getting there would not be easy. Pilar was a most inhospitable den mother, her deadpan scowl spray-painted on while she pointed an accusatory finger flashing chipped polish and told us bluntly: *I house you for the money*. She repeated that phrase throughout the day, yelling in a deep, raspy smoker's voice and gesticulating angrily with an added foot stomp. We dreaded this special voice, acquired by years of lazing all day long in her perpetual outfit, a nightgown, on her yellow, floral sofa in front of the tv, lighting one cigarette after another, breaking only to curse at a telenovela villain.

We ate the same meals three times a day for three months. She packed cold tortilla fritas we ate during our thirty minute walk to school, bodega sandwiches for lunch, and at five P.M., dinner back at her house. I never knew what we were eating. Christie and I sat at a small, round table in Pilar's living room while she observed us from the couch, making sure we ate everything. Waste was not an option. We practiced our Spanish by attempting to engage her in conversation during the local news broadcast, believing we could jump right into her side commentary full of obscenities at the news anchors, but we remained unanswered.

She was obsessed with her water supply, allowing us only two minutes to shower. If we exceeded the time limit, she knocked loudly on the door yelling *VAMANOS,* prompting her scrawny, bald, blind dog to bark.

A brighter prospect than Pilar was Semana Santa *Holy Week,* a highlight of the trip. Parades with giant floats festooned the brick-paved streets. Local families assembled in churches, celebrating with food, drink, and music. Traveling throughout Europe, I visited some of the most exquisite churches, which people traveled from all over the world to see for their extraordinary structures and for their ethereal spaces. I lit a candle and sat in silence inhaling the air and energy around me and praying. I prayed to feel unconflicted in God's presence. I felt a degree of disharmony because we partied daily, and although I craved spirituality, feeling it was difficult when I was waking up every day hungover. Maybe that was spirituality, right there, recognizing the conflict. I knew I wanted to somehow soak myself in its comfort.

SPIRITUAL ADVENTURE NUMBER THREE

Meeting men from all over the world at night clubs was a scary adventure, unpredictable and risky. Going to see Bruce Springsteen in Barcelona, where few knew English but knew every word of "Born in the USA" was surprising. Hiking Cinque Terre in Italy was awesome. The Red Light District in Amsterdam was intriguing. The Basilicas and the Eiffel Tower were stupendous. Men wanting to cut my bleached blond hair for sale in Morocco was novel, and topless beaches in The Algarve were exotic and luxurious. The Berlin Wall, London, and Ireland were all dream-like. The whole semester felt mystical, and I was proud of the life choices I had made thus far.

Returning from my *Alice in Wonderland* adventures was a test in transitioning. I was walking in clouds, my thoughts swirls of fantastical memories of friends I had made from all over the world. I was still living in full color history on a high and wanting not to come down from it. But I did, and the process was no gradual detox but absolute cold turkey.

Al's aggressive, dismissive commentary was a shock to my system. I may as well have crashed my head into a brick wall. Feeling over the moon to share my experiences with him, photo album in my hand, his response was, *How much money did you spend on this trip? All of these pictures of you are in taverns. You could have saved a lot of money if you'd stayed right here and done a pub-crawl every weekend throughout all of the Chicago neighborhoods and pretended you were in Europe. There's a lot of culture to be seen in Chicago, too.* Pure rage consumed me and then shame, because maybe he was right, and I never realized until many years later that devaluing my experience was the only way for him to appease his insecurity, to quash his own dreams. I vowed not to let him extinguish mine.

SPIRITUAL ADVENTURE NUMBER FOUR

I was still young, in my early twenties. I'd learned that the church of the grade school I attended, down the street from the bar, was hosting a trip to San Salvador, the capital of El Salvador, Florentine's home. I hungered for more time out from the world, and I signed up. San Salvador was gang infested, the schools lacked even the most basic of resources, and the mountain homes were made of clay with no running water, and there were no bathrooms, only buckets. Tiendas made of straw were strewn along the railroad tracks, selling ten cent sodas in straw-plugged plastic bags. The pace of life was relaxed, slow. Buses were unhurried, the rides consuming hours spent discussing life with nine other adults twice my age.

I've been known to have a familiar old soul and an ability to connect with anyone, regardless of age, a trait invaluable to me in my practice of life diversity. I learned that these families lived close to each other, often on the same street. They recounted stories about their never-ending porch talks. Life was simple: for example, I observed mothers washing their babies in local streams. The importance in their daily existence was eye contact and saying hello and good morning. The most fitting word to describe their way of life is civilized, a quality missing from most of the world today.

Cusco, Peru, the wealthiest of the three cities in Central and South America that I visited, was breathtakingly beautiful. The town shut down for siesta two hours each day, people heading home for the nap or for lunch with their families. A primary source of revenue was the tourism of Machu Picchu. There, I met up with Kate, who lived there for volunteer work. With backpacks higher than we were, we hiked four days, each route more beautiful than the previous one. We slept in tents along the trail under those distant stars of glory I still reached for, and we were awakened at dawn by guides proffering little cups of CoCo tea.

The adventure proved more challenging than any marathon I had ever run. After one day of hiking eight hours and feeling beaten up, bruised, and fatigued beyond belief, we got up and did it all over again three more times. Mornings were cold and wet, but by afternoon the sun beat down on our backs and faces. The journey was worth every mile of the trip: the summit greeted us with sacred, ancient Inca ruins. In that awesome moment, I felt like a tiny spec in the universe.

We moved on to party at a bar along the trail with other hikers. I was in heaven: booze, exercise, adventure, Spanish language, and friendship—all of my core values at the time.

On our last day, we began our initial descent, brutal on the knees and equally brutal on the will to champion. When we reached the bottom, we felt victorious. We had done it; We had hiked Machu Picchu. Kate and I fell exhausted into each other's arms and cried tears of joy: we had experienced one of the Seven Wonders of the World together. *God Wink.*

Hot, hotel showers, heaps of food, massages, and sleeping in a bed for twelve hours—the simple things in life—renewed us, and we returned to Lima, where Kate snuck me into her host family's home, that is, snuck me on top of their home. We slept on their low flat roof under those stars before heading to the airport. After six days, my journey had suddenly ended and had returned me to reality. I tried to hold on to my experience, to my spiritual infilling, treasuring my fresh intimacy with God, which had put my life into perspective. I wanted to share my gratitude and joy with friends and family now.

It was short-lived. I found myself back on the familiar, daily merry-go-round, returned to the same old rat race unable to articulate this new feeling, this new way of life, almost like trying to speak a new language alien to fellow American, Chicago friends and family. I longed for my next binge on God and his awesome universe and for empowerment to glorify him rather than the poverty I witnessed, the fact that many of those people want, lack, need, more, relief from crime, alcoholism, prostitution, and disease. I want to share that sense of peace come over me, the power far greater than myself moving through my vessel. It's the feeling that hits me when I feel connected to humanity, too: *Listening. A gentle touch. A warm hug. Staying grounded. Revering nature. Moving to help out . . .*

I've also had powerful ritualistic experiences of connection around organized religion of every denomination. Curiosity is what keeps me seeking and engaged. Often, when I ask someone, *How would you describe your spirituality,* he or she usually responds with, *Oh, I'm not religious at all,* or with, *I was raised Catholic but organized religion turns me off.* I'm always motivated by the opportunity to use this teaching moment to explain the difference between religion and spirituality. You can have one without the other. You can have both. You choose.

SPIRITUALITY

Where do I find Meaning?

How do I feel Connected?

How do I want to Live?

Spirituality is the process of personal transformation and exploration. Prayer is talking; meditation is listening. There can be an overlap of religion and spirituality, which are not mutually exclusive, but which may exist without the other, separate entities. Some people identify themselves as spiritual, some religious, some both, some none. I have found no precise formula. Be open-minded, and wear every experience like a loose garment easily shed. At least, this credo has worked for me.

RELIGION

What practices, rites, or rituals "should" I follow?

What is true and false?

What is right and wrong?

Religion is an organized, structured way to connect with God and to put our faith into action. As someone who struggles with rules, I often feel ashamed when I break the rules. I confessed to premarital sex with my long term boyfriend at Reconciliation in high school, and the priest told me that if I was really sorry, I wouldn't do it again.

I guess I wasn't really that sorry.

I struggled to feel *good enough* in the eyes of the church. At an early age, I learned about a judgmental God I either wanted to please or to hide from, as though he were keeping a tally board in heaven. Thus, I became more comfortable as a Cafeteria Catholic, choosing what felt right and forsaking the rest. I identify as someone with a strong connection to many different convictions rooted in spiritual practice. If we want a spiritual foundation, we need to work at it daily. Here are some suggestions and activities I engage in to strengthen my understanding of something greater than myself. I hope this will help you get started as you begin or continue to explore your deeper understanding of spirituality.

I. *Being emotionally intimate and vulnerable in my relationships.*

II. *Sitting by the ocean awakening my senses—listening to the waves, seeing the beauty, smelling the air, feeling the sun and wind on my face. This is when I truly feel alive.*

III. *Traveling, learning about other cultures, serving others, experiential learning.*

IV. *Deep breathing.*

V. *Writing.*

VI. *Listening to music and connecting with the words and rhythm as it vibrates throughout my body.*

It's taken me decades to learn to be gentle with myself, to simply BE *myself*. This practice has slowed me down and granted me greater all around life experiences; a greater connection with myself, others, and to something bigger than all of us.

VIII
RELIGION

S ymbolism is strong for me, a trinket, for example, something that speaks to me. I like to use humor, and I treasure my Roller Derby Jesus figurine that was a gift, maybe one of the best. Roller Derby Jesus had been my travel companion through all of my expeditions, reposing proudly on the dashboard during road trips and stuffed snugly in my backpack during the Machu Picchu trek. When the altitude or exhaustion played tricks on my mind, Roller Derby Jesus and I had a little talk. Other symbols I collect like relics are coffee mugs with inspirational quotes and angels, who adorn a special shelf. Other symbols are tattooed on my arm to remind me how far I've come so that I never forget my journey.

I am reminded of strength and hope. I have a plaque on my bookshelf next to all of my favorite books: *Lord, keep your arm around my shoulder and your hand over my mouth from A Reflection on Common Sins of Speech* by Msgr. Charles Pope. The prayer reminds me not to be so reactive with words. I've been known to fly off the handle when pushed to extreme anger. I've had to learn that, most of the time, the most effective tool is to say less and to listen more. It's not an exact science and requires practice, because I enjoy talking.

I often initiate conversation with people when I'm in public, trying always to keep my eyes open to new encounters. On one particular day, I visited a park in Santa Monica with my children and saw three beautiful multiracial children. My curiosity was piqued about their ethnicity, but I was hesitant to ask their mother, wanting not to offend her and because I was working on my listening more and talking less skills. I took the risk. She was open and appreciative and allowed conversation. She told me the children were Persian and African-American. She said her religion was called *Bahai,* a progressive philosophy encouraging interracial marriage. She thanked me for asking about them. We discussed the importance of awareness of other cultures and religions in order to avoid ignorance and prejudice.

THE CLEANING LADY

It was Labor Day weekend, and we let the household chores slide that entire week due to pure exhaustion from our work schedules. My neighbor recommended a cleaning lady, something I was unaccustomed to in adulthood but needed, desperate to return home to a clean house every day; I called right away. My savior arrived with broken English and with a twenty year old daughter in tow. We left the house to get out of their way, and when we got home the house was immaculate. We could have eaten dinner off the bathroom floor. The ladies had scrubbed for seeming eternity, and it was late. I didn't want them enduring a ninety minute bus ride, so I made it clear I'd drive them home.

The daughter got into my car and said, *Wow, this is really nice.* My internal dialogue was, This Chevy? *Oh gosh, please don't be envious, I was fortunate enough to be gifted this lease from my father-in-law. I certainly couldn't afford it on my own.* The Chevy was absolutely devoid of bells or whistles, but to someone else, it was a limousine. I was fortunate to have a car. I realized another appreciation of a simple thing easily taken for granted.

I witnessed an area of east Los Angeles that I was unaware existed. On our twenty minute commute, the daughter opened up and told me about Mexican culture, family, viewpoints on marriage and religion, and about what she aspired to professionally, no longer the same girl who had walked into my house shy and hardly capable of making eye contact. I couldn't believe the sacrifices their family had made by emigrating to the States for a better life. In American culture, a family of five living in a two bedroom apartment and traveling hours by bus to make a living might be looked at as a sad life. These women were grateful for the opportunities they had been given as immigrants, just like Florentino. Their life was happy and blessed, defying one's preconceived notion.

In high school, I volunteered at a residential HIV/AIDS facility in Lincoln Park. I was the youngest volunteer, and I had the opportunity to meet and interact with people drug- addicted or prostituting or gay, all of them with multiple unprotected sex partners. I found myself more comfortable around people overtly hurting and seeming ready and willing to connect and to be authentic. They shared their hopes and fears with me with openness and courage, but I was unable yet to articulate my hopes and fears or or to reveal my own pain.

Many had lost family members due to their lifestyle choices or had been rejected because of their illnesses. This community leaned on each other and fostered camaraderie and hope. One of the house members invited me to attend a nondenominational religious service with her. She disclosed her life story and how she had contracted the AIDS virus. *I had seven minutes of pleasure, which has caused me seven years of pain.* Many people at the church were homeless, broke, mentally ill, and struggling with quivers of personal demons yet showed up Sundays to worship and to feel the comforting sense of belonging. I was moved by the warm welcome and by their embrace. There was no judging.

I've been invited to several African-American Baptist churches throughout the country— on the South Side of Chicago, in Sunnyvale and Santa Monica, California. The only white person in the congregation,

I never felt out of place. I was struck by the passion and excitement emanating during several hours of worship. People didn't just cry—they wept! They sang from the rock bottom of their hearts; they felt the spirit move them; they fell on their knees and prayed and listened with every fiber of their being to the words preached; and I soaked it all in, too, the challenges and assurances fortifying and encouraging me so that I returned frequently when I felt I was sinking low, so that the atmosphere breathed life into me like the purest, perfect, spiritual fix.

STRIVING FOR BUDDHISM

Growing up in a primarily Catholic environment, I had little exposure to Judaism, either culturally or religiously. I moved to Los Angeles and worked at a Women's Counseling Center under the auspices of the National Council of Jewish Women. As a guidance counselor at a Catholic high school, I taught Hebrew Scriptures and the Old Testament. Christianity and Judaism are so interrelated, yet we try to keep them separated. I've been impressed by a tight knit, powerful community enriched by a shared history.

I've visited a mosque. I covered my head to attend and sat in the back like all other women and observed. The rituals of prayer and the chanting, rhythmic and lyrical, soothed me. There was unity and a calming aura despite the fact that men were in control, which was accepted without question, assuring no conflict. I strive for a Buddhist sensibility: to learn the right way of living; to be awakened; to practice mindfulness and meditation in hope of reaching Nirvana; referring to the composed stillness of mind after the fires of desire, aversion, and delusion have finally been eradicated.

I'm a Cafeteria Catholic, I'm Buddha-inspired, and I worship with my sisters at a nondenominational Christian church with a rock star band called Soul City—a true community with a whole lot of deep soul. *I raise my hands in the air like I just don't care* and sing loudly at the top of my lungs. I feel goosebumps throughout the whole one hour experience, a guarantee I feel enlightened to start my week. I'm more spiritual-minded than religious, choosing what works for me and enjoying putting my faith into action with rituals such as Baptism, Communion, Easter, and Christmas. I use an eclectic approach in the way I choose to worship by building a non-blaming, non-shaming foundation; I don't want to be identified or labeled as committing to any one single religion.

We've got to stop *shoulding* ourselves, creating feelings of guilt. I *should have* gone to church today; I should have called to let someone know I was thinking of them. We will be left with nothing but regret and feeling bad about ourselves. I *could have* gone to that baby shower, but I chose not to. We

but substituting material objects for emotional needs requires adjustment.

I'm amazed and envious of people who stay at the same job for thirty years. They live in the same house, where they raised their kids in the same routine day after day in apparent contentment. That lifestyle worked for my grandparents, whom I admired and adored. Married for fifty-seven years, they stayed in the same small town where Grandpa worked and Grandma stayed home with four kids. Keeping to their assigned roles was a great source of their happiness. They exemplified love, commitment, and selflessness to our entire family.

THE STAIRS

The Santa Monica stairs are a grueling hotspot set of one hundred and seventy wooden stairs that never seem to end. We torture ourselves and do it over and over again until our breathing is labored and our legs are shaking. Some people turn on their iTunes, pull their tinted Chanel glasses over their eyes, and further conceal their faces with wide brimmed hats. Once they're incognito, they take off as if they are the one and only person attempting this challenge. If you initiate it when you are going up and other people are going down, you may get a smile from someone acknowledging that he or she, too, felt the pain and the tears of perspiration. I try to push the envelope; it's my nature. I encourage people as I pass them, give a little woo-hoo, and give myself one when I get to the top as I complete each brutal set. On one steamy summer day, the temperature was still rising. A man quite my senior zoomed past me as though he were merely skipping effortlessly through his house. When we reached the top and broke for water, I said, *You are amazing!* I asked how old he was, and he said seventy-three. He said he was not amazing and explained he did what he could and strived to do his best every day. He credited his empowerment to God, who chose his path. And he was a little angel crossing my path that day. *God wink.*

7-11

It was raining, a relentless torrential downpour. I was in a rush and had two small children in tow. The familiar 7-Eleven sign beckoned me as I careened into the parking lot. I wrangled the kids from their car seats and schlepped them inside. They sprinted immediately down the candy aisle and delivered their treasured treats to the counter while I checked out my newspaper and a gallon of milk. The store was packed, and a few rude persons bumped right into others with no seeming regard for personal space. I was sure we were going to piss somebody off. The deluge threatened outside, and impatient glares menaced inside. Returning to the car, feeling relieved I was no longer inconveniencing other patrons, a woman in the parking lot approached and said, *Those children are beautiful; enjoy them while they are young, because it goes by so fast.* Her words surprised me, the opposite of my expectations, my guard up ready to defend the difficulty of parenting for me. I reset, breathed deeply, and shifted my perspective. *God wink.*

I learned in that moment to open my eyes to daily chance encounters and to appreciate random acts of strangers. We all have this ability if we allow ourselves to claim it, and it's magical: slowing down helps me to listen to what the world, my children, and relationships are trying to tell me. When I'm unaware of the possibility of emotionally or spiritually rewarding serendipitous encounters, my husband, Ryan, is a genius at reeling me in by *reminding me,* even if he needs to repeat himself ten times before I'm back.

I X

DARKNESS

The time was nine thirty on one exceptionally humid Chicago May night. I had one year left of undergraduate study, and for my tuition, I spent the summer working as a cocktail waitress in an outdoor beer garden in the Southport Corridor in Lakeview. It's a primarily Caucasian middle to upper class neighborhood of young families and neighborhood bars. I left early that night because business was slow; my boyfriend at the time, Ryan, now my husband, usually picked me up so I never had to walk alone late at night. The walk home was only a few short blocks, and I wanted to surprise him so that we could spend some time together. I wore a simple black dress with ballet flats, my apron folded and in one hand, a hundred dollars in cash tucked away. Some people relaxed on their porches, drinking, and others enjoyed a walk on this muggy, late spring night. I looked forward to doing the same.

Turning off the main drag onto my street, it was unusually dark and quiet. I was halfway down the block when a short Latino man hardly taller than I, about 5'3", walked toward me. My heart pounded in alarm.

My mouth turned dry, and my hands and ankles felt cold and clammy. I considered crossing the street but didn't want him to sense my fear. I'd learned in self-defense class to look directly into someone else's eyes to show you are alert and unafraid. I did exactly that, although I was, indeed, afraid.

We locked eyes, and he came closer and suddenly blocked me. He thrust his arm out with a blow to my neck hard enough to throw me to the concrete on my back. The wind knocked out of me, I could barely breathe, but I fought desperately for my life. I clawed his face and screamed at the top of my voice, but the effort sounded like rasping whispers. I kicked and tried pushing him off me, but he pinned me down and lifted my black cotton Gap dress and shoved his fist into my vagina, inducing bleeding and urinating all over myself. His long fingernails, probably filthy, scraped inside me, and the smell of soaking sweat arose from both of us. His minutes seemed like an eternity. Believing he was going to kill me, I contemplated playing dead, and I closed my eyes, anyway, praying for this assault to end.

The loud noise of a dumpster top slamming down on metal prompted him to sprint down the alley. Now in shock, I kicked off my black ballet flats and ran barefoot as fast as I could, although it felt like I was running through deep water, and my ankles kept knocking into each other, tripping me.

I made it to the closest business I could find, a bar gloriously filled with other people, and I arrived crying, shaking, and struggling to articulate my needs. I was inaudible but for choking sobs. People stared, speechless. I made my way to the bar and asked for the phone. The bartender gave me a glass of water and a cigarette and told me to calm down. I called Ryan, who rushed immediately to me, flagging down a police car along the way.

Two male officers arrived and approached me and asked if I had been drinking. They doubted me, seemingly blaming me for the attack. Finally, they asked if I wanted a ride home. I was unsure what I wanted. I decided to ask to be driven to the hospital, because I hadn't been drinking; I had been working. I kept repeating those words: *I was working . . . not drinking.* I lit the smoke the bartender gave me, and the officer curtly informed me he was no taxi driver and that I needed to put out my cigarette and to get in the car. He drove us to the nearest hospital, and we waited in the Emergency Room for what seemed like another eternity but which was only an hour. I felt paranoid with everyone glancing at me, but I also wanted to tell everyone what had happened so that other women could protect themselves.

A different officer interrogated me, asking me to describe what the attacker looked like, needing a rough sketch to see if he could match the composite to any other known attackers. There had recently been a string of similar crimes in the neighborhood. This officer was slightly kinder and more sympathetic but seemed quite annoyed at the late event keeping his shift from ending.

I registered at the hospital, always an irritating, daunting task, and was taken to an exam room where a male doctor (I had thought my case should have provided a female) and a Rape Victim Advocate greeted me. RVA provides throughout Chicago area Emergency Rooms non-judgmental emotional support to survivors of sexual violence. The doctor used a rape kit, consisting of my clothes bagged for evidence, an internal exam, and an oral swab. The advocate educated me about what to expect in the aftermath and continued to reiterate that *it was not your fault.* She provided me with resources for my healing process, which included eight free therapy sessions at RVA, just enough to get the process started. I wanted to begin immediately, but there was a long waiting list.

I was unaware Ryan had called Mom, my cavalry, for extra support. I needed her. She is rock solid during a crisis, a Rock of Gibraltar. Despite her presence this night, however, arriving home was bittersweet. I desired the safety of my own home, my own bed, my own blankets, Ryan . . . but I didn't feel safe; I couldn't shake the overwhelming violation to my skin, which I felt crawled inside and outside with filth. I wanted to shower, but I was afraid to be alone. The thought of being alone slowed my breathing until I froze in place. I lived only a few short blocks from the incident and was petrified that the attacker would return for me, that he knew where I lived and that he was always watching or would be watching now. Ryan was patient. He held me in the shower while I cried that evening and many subsequent evenings. My physical and emotional pain was unfathomable to him, and he told me he felt frustrated that there was nothing he could do to protect me or to make me feel safer.

I never slept that night or many subsequent nights, replaying the incident over and over, beating myself up with regret that I had refused to listen to my damn gut about crossing the street. The incident could have been avoided if I had just acted on my intuition, but now were nightmares about him breaking the door down or climbing through the window. I saw him in dark corners, his shadow on the wall opposite my bed. I tried to reassure myself by trivializing the attack in my head, thinking, *It was only sexual assault; I got away this time.* But was he feeling like a failure? Would he want to complete his job with penetration in order to call it *rape?*

I learned that rape is not about sex; it's about power and control in an act of violence. I stayed in the same clothes for days and never left the house and never ate. I felt like nobody understood. All I heard was, *Stop feeling sorry for yourself; you need to get back to life,* and, *You'll get through this.* Maybe they thought these words would empower me, but they did just the opposite. I felt rage because they didn't understand, because I was

93

scared, and because I felt powerless. I tried avoiding Al, because I was embarrassed. When I did see him, he empathized by telling me he knew how I felt because he had gotten a gun pulled on him once. I know he harbored good intentions and tried to relate, but I would personally have preferred a pointing gun to a stabbing, stray penis.

I needed to get away from Chicago, and Ryan and I had been tossing around the idea of going to the Jersey Shore to visit his family. I hadn't yet been introduced, and naturally I was slightly apprehensive, but an absolute need to heal overpowered apprehension. A week later, we were packed and en route. As the trip progressed, my shoulders began relaxing, my breathing slackened, my legs quit skittering, my toes quit tapping compulsively. The knowledge I was headed somewhere unknown to the attacker was like a permeating balm, and I began to feel liberated from danger, *safe*.

The shore became a safe haven for me and a sacred place and continues to be sixteen years later. Ryan's family were welcoming and empathic, polar opposites to life with Al. I struggled to keep myself together. Moments of acceptance and of clarity and even of joy soon receded to panic, anxiety and supreme sadness, precluding the best presentation of myself. We stretched out on the beach, and I thrived in the purifying ocean air, feeling a bit closer to heaven. This cocoon in which I had ensconced myself, however, became a trap of sorts. I felt loved and cared for and *safe,* but now I was uncertain how to re-enter the game of life.

After much thought, I decided to go back to work. My return was auspicious, but the entire kitchen staff was Latino, and every time I saw a guy who looked Latino, I panicked, thinking that *he* was the attacker. When I concluded that one of the guys from the kitchen may have followed me home that night, I quit.

I wondered whether moving to a different neighborhood with a security system would make me feel safe. It helped a little, but I became entirely dependent on Ryan. I couldn't be alone or park my car on the street unless it was directly in front of my house, and I ran everywhere because being around crowds overwhelmed me with threatening men resembling my attacker. I was diagnosed with PTSD (Post Traumatic Stress Disorder) and lived in fear for almost a year whether awake or asleep. I desperately wanted a *How To Overcome Sexual Assault in Six Weeks* manual to move past this crisis and get on with my life. Unable to find one, I listened to internal desires.

I consumed alcohol most nights to numb my mind, to reduce sudden startling, and to sleep without nightmares, hopefully. I also participated in women's survivor groups and began individual therapy with a sexual assault specialist. I read *After the Silence, Rape and My Journey Back* by Nancy Venable Raine. She describes the inability to think or fight our way out of this hell. We must feel our way and tell our story to recover.

All I had were my words, and I needed to work hard to reclaim and to reconstruct myself. I became motivated to champion for myself and for other female survivors of sexual assault. I wanted not to feel ashamed.

Alderman meetings were held throughout the city to try to enhance positive police involvement and safety in the neighborhoods on the North Side of Chicago. I attended and spoke at the meetings, hoping to make a difference by sharing my experience. The attacks were an epidemic every year at the start of summer, the dominant prey young women around major universities. The news broadcasts covered the same, sorry story of dozens of women assaulted, the pattern one of instilling fear until women turned wary, creating a brief lull in the attacks until the cycle repeated itself. Detectives sought a link between one attacker scenario and all the women attacked that summer, producing sketches of potential young male Latino suspects with rap sheets. None of them matched my attacker; we still had nothing.

Daily corrective experiences of feeling safe, my treatment, and a supportive relationship with Ryan were the major contributors to my healing. Our physical touch and sexual intimacy were put on hold until I felt more at peace within my body. One therapist cautioned me about the high risk to longevity of intimate relationships after an assault, because the recovery becomes too intense for the supporting partner. I anticipated Ryan walking away, becoming sure of it and practically willing it to happen, yet he continued to show up. He attended therapy with me and supported me, although, at times, he became understandably frustrated with my behavior and general state of well-being. But we worked through it together.

Ryan's continuous support and positive outlook effectively enabled my free spirit and helped me conquer this trauma. That doesn't mean I'm carefree or free from fear. I am still cautious and alert to my surroundings, and I still have a strong startle response when someone sneaks up on me. When I'm alone in the parking garage at six A.M., I always glance around and scan the space, my keys between my fingers, my thumb poised to press the panic button. In an elevator, if I'm alone with a strange man, the issue of safety crosses my mind. I no longer stroll dark streets or walk with headphones on. Only an oblivious, vulnerable target texts when walking down the street.

I encourage women to be more aware of their surroundings when alone. I was angry with the universe that night and for months following. I felt that God had neglected to protect me. I kept asking *Why me?* I'm still careful, still on high alert, but I'm in control of these choices and will no longer allow fear to inhibit me. I guess what doesn't kill us does make us stronger. Resentment was a huge obstacle, but I have finally forgiven him—and, more importantly, I have forgiven *myself.* According to RAINN (Rape Abuse and Incest National Network), every one hundred and seven seconds, an American is sexually assaulted. We need to become more aware and to watch out for one another.

I contribute to many national publications on topics such as "Enhancing Your Sex Life" or "Women Need To Masturbate, Too." In my practice, I treat men who are sex addicts, I work with couples in sexually starved marriages, and I help women become more comfortable with their bodies and with their sexuality. Sexuality is a very important issue in my career. I've worked through not one but two sexual traumas, and I have a sexually fulfilling relationship with my partner—and with *myself.* Therapists aren't always right, another lesson to learn in beating the odds. Everyone deserves a healthy and comfortable relationship with sexuality, but particularly in spite of any past trauma. *It is never your fault.*

X

FAMILY, ANXIETY, IUD'S & LIFE

When I met Ryan in 1999, he was a Friday night regular at the bar. He and his friend, both from Jersey, ordered only Miller Light and Budweiser, and after a little flirtatious banter, headed for the jukebox to play *everything* Bruce Springsteen. I thought he was cute, and his sense of humor and sardonic views were added benefits. I was unable to like his wardrobe, however, hardly ideal for my taste: his customary attire was a spring break Baja beach jacket, black Ankle Biter jeans, a slightly feathered mullet, and black combat boots. Maybe it was the Baja beach jacket I had a problem with. Before long, I learned this fashion dragon was an actor trying to get his start here in Chicago. That explained it.

Roughly once a week for a year, Jersey Buddy and Ryan sat at the bar. We'd shoot the shit while I fed them free beer and shots. In return, I heard about all of the outrageous experiences of being single in Chicago. I was, and still am, wildly attracted to his artistic nature, free spirit, love for family and for the beach, patience, laid back nature, ability to never give up, and belief that all ends up working out. He has shown me over and over again that, indeed, it does.

We first developed a friendship after discovering that BK attended college with his sister. I began to trust him and found myself looking forward to seeing him at the bar. One Friday night, he entered without Jersey Buddy but with a girl instead. I stood behind the bar, about to get him a drink, but my heart sank, and I felt like a blatant fool. I wondered if I had been indulging a fantasy, because clearly we weren't on the same page. I had convinced myself before work to ask him out that night. Apparently, however, I still might be in luck: the date was apparently not going well, and when serendipity sent her to the bathroom, Ryan asked if I was free over the weekend. My guard up, I sassed him a bit and asked what had taken him so long! I was elated, literally over the moon, practically jumping up and down inside, but I played it cool.

I drove to his house late the next morning and picked him up in my brown, two door Mazda Protege with no power steering. Our date was lunch at John's Place, a neighborhood cafe, casual, easy, and entertaining. We clicked. I couldn't stop smiling. I'm sure he questioned my sanity in those moments, the perpetual smile and constant laughing a bit over the top, the butterflies in my stomach clearly overcaffeinated. When I dropped him off, he leaned over, studied my eyes, and passionately kissed me before opening the door.

The moment I stepped inside my house, I called Kate and said, "You know that song by Vertical Horizon? *He's everything you want . . . he's everything you need . . . he's everything inside of you that you wish you could be . . . he says all the right things at exactly the right time . . .* that's how I feel about that regular guy from the bar!"

I quickly became attached to him and wanted to spend every moment with him, which soon became a reality. I indulged an impulse to buy a puppy four months into our relatively new relationship, neglecting to inform my roommates, who ultimately gave me the boot. I moved in with Ryan and his college roommate, who had gone to the all boys high school down the street from my all girls high school. Although six years my senior, we had several mutual friends, and the familiarity put me at ease after my puppy binge and particularly after breaching his territory, which was quite a relief. Another serendipitous encounter, or another God wink?

We spent most of our dating career basically socializing, an abundance of hanging out at neighborhood bars and drinking and listening to music and meeting up with friends. We were always up to partying.

The assault happened only a month after moving in with Ryan, forcing a quick end to the honeymoon. Our relationship went from playtime to intensity to a trusting relationship to one threatened by sudden vulnerability. The next few years, we were on again/off again. I constantly pushed him away, little shoves here and there, and eventually moved to another state to pursue more adventures. I was unable to persuade him to join me. I knew I desperately wanted to marry him, but he wasn't yet ready, and I wasn't one to dally, to let matters slide until finally panning out. When I wanted something, anything, I went after it ferociously, the word no alien to my thinking. I pursued my goal until I got what I wanted. This time I didn't, however, although the wait defied my nature. I managed to back off but remained in contact, always hoping. I loved Ryan's family and visited them even during our break ups. We became especially close during my time in New Hampshire working at an all boys residential treatment facility. I was also close to his sister whom BK attended college with, and another sister asked me to become the godparent for her son. They were the family I had always longed for and had always wanted to be a part of, because I felt welcomed, loved, and safe.

Dad's core values instilled independence. In his view, self-sufficiency was the only way to be strong; leaning on anyone else for anything was a sign of weakness. That creed was challenged by a relationship with someone like Ryan, who welcomed the chance to be my knight in shining armor. How does someone as strong-willed as myself convincingly play the damsel in distress? Ryan has patiently tolerated the conflict this sensibility caused over the years and has taught me to lean on him and on others. Asking for help is not a sign of weakness.

After graduating from my Masters program, I wanted to move to Santa Monica. I hungered for the soothing sunshine and for palm tree views. Initially, Ryan was unenthused, and we went round in circles. We worked diligently through some of the turmoil I'd brought into the relationship, no easy feat. I am a handful, I admit. He knew what he was getting into when he asked me to marry him. He hadn't planned to propose, but he popped the question while we headed out for a run. He proffered no ring, no bowed knee, no flute of champagne or stein of beer; he simply said, right to the point, cool, calm, and collected, "Hey, you wanna get married?" Within five months, we sold everything, married, and headed to sunny southern California.

I have heard it said that you end up marrying someone whose behavior and possibly even physical attributes resemble your opposite sex parent. In my case, that adage couldn't be farther from the truth except for the fact that he, like Al, marches to the beat of his own drum, a trait I'm grateful for. There is however, a striking resemblance and love for exercise and the beach between his four sisters and me!

In October 2004, we married in a beach ceremony at the Jersey Shore. We invited only those closest to us, and our guests packed into a pavilion overlooking the Atlantic. We recruited an acoustic folk guitar player and his wife for musicians. We wrote our own vows, and Kate officiated after convincing my devout Catholic in-laws that she was ordained—no lie, although she had obtained an online certificate. Kate gave a homily about how opposites attract. *Ryan keeps Kelley grounded. Bottom line.* Friends and family experienced a place I loved and cherished, a place that had been and always will be my safe haven. Our reception was at our favorite bar at the shore, and we ate the best seafood and danced the night away to our wedding song, "Somewhere Over the Rainbow" by the Hawaiian singer IZ.

After the weekend of wedding festivities, we drove back to Chicago to catch a flight to the Dominican Republic for our official honeymoon, the start of our endless vacation considering we were flying home after the trip, packing the car, and hauling ourselves cross-country to Santa Monica, both jobless. Drinks and dinner at a bar in the neighborhood of Andersonville kept us out until two A.M. Our flight was scheduled to take off at six A.M., but, unsurprisingly, we overslept. We didn't make the flight out that day, and there was actually only one flight every day. Frantic, we charmed Customer Service and by evening finagled a flight to Santo Domingo. We found our way to a dark and dingy motel and slept in our clothes in a room with a cockroach family in the tub.

At sunrise, we endured a five hour taxi ride through washboard back roads to our resort. This beginning of our journey together turned out to become symbolic of the many other bumps and winding twists and turns lying ahead. Finally arriving, we defused and focused on each other for the next five days, enjoying a relaxing vacation at a beautiful resort. Naturally, we became best friends of the bartenders, never shedding our bathing suits. Life was a beach, calm waves before mounting storm. There always seems to be ghostly tranquility before sudden chaos. The loud, chopping rhythm of the helicopter propellers, hypnotic like slow motion, and the gentle glide over the turquoise sea were eerily soothing, temporary vacation thrills unlikely to last, seeming like a warning about the newness of the life we were about to build together. I managed to keep my expectations high, however, and within twenty-four hours we were back in Chicago, a stark contrast to our beach bar in the Dominican Republic, and a brief stop before our pioneer trek to California.

We loaded our wagon and met along the way to California a wide range of vastly different people and shared enriching conversations with them. Four days later on Halloween, we arrived in Santa Monica and planted ourselves in our tiny one bedroom apartment seven blocks from the ocean, which is considered prime real estate. Seven blocks only? Unbelievable, but we had needed a home immediately and had flown to LA a few weeks prior to sign a lease, pleading with prospective, selective landlords bombarded with forty applicants to rent to us. Persistence and good old-fashioned Jersey charm won when Ryan told the owners he wanted to surprise me with the apartment for our wedding gift. Every bride wanted and would highly prize a new home in which to begin a new life together. We hit the jackpot, and the landlords took us in like family. God knows we needed one. They lived on the property in the larger house in front of us with their four children and invited us to Mexican family fiestas on Sundays, where we toasted to good health with very strong tequila.

It felt like we were on solid ground. We were ambitious and conscientiously bent on diving into our careers. I went to numerous interviews and Ryan to auditions, but the competition in and around L.A. for therapists and actors is staggering, absolutely disheartening and discouraging. Thus, we took timeouts from the rat race and rode beach cruisers on the Strand, breaking at beachfront bars to guzzle from tall steins German beer until the Pacific sunset. We splurged at incredible restaurants, living off the monetary gifts and riches from our wedding. We felt as though we were living the dream, and a few months of beach life went by before the routine became a rut. We realized we were going nowhere fast. I wanted to give up, to quit trying, and to move back to Chicago. Ryan was landing acting gigs in commercials, plays, and independent films, but he was a very small fish in a gigantic pond. We were barely paying the bills. There seemed to be no way out, although I worked as an independent contractor at three different facilities, earning clinical hours in order to sit for my licensing exam, which had the reputation of being the hardest in the country. I passed. I began to feel more optimistic about the decision to live on the West Coast. We still continued to struggle, however, day after day, but we made it work by considering ourselves fortunate to live life in the sun.

Within the first year, I was pregnant with our first child, not *yet* part of the plan. The itch to move back to Chicago became strong again. I wanted familiarity. I wanted my sisters close when I became a mom. We could barely afford living in Santa Monica as a twosome; how would we pull it off as a threesome? My pattern in life when life got hard had always been to change external environments in the hope that I'd feel more content. In other words, my pattern had always been to run. I'm a runner. The problem is I was always discontent and insecure with *myself,* who never unloaded, which meant the change of venue was a temporary fix. I needed to work on calming my inner dialogue and on being content with where I was at that time. Ryan encouraged us to push through rather than give up, reminding me of all the family and friends who loved to come out and visit. He was also ambitious and knew it wasn't yet time for us to leave. Again, the race was on. I needed to figure myself out and to work out all of the kinks. That was ten years ago, and sometimes I still feel as though I have some figuring out to do.

I know few people in my personal or professional life who have said, "Okay, I think we're ready to have a baby. We both have good jobs, a home we own, a lump of money in checking and savings; bring it on." Doesn't everyone have that initial fear? We were conflicted because we were both terrified and elated, two extremes with no middle ground. Every facet of our lives was extreme, the pressure sometimes causing you to lose objectivity. Always racing from one job to the next was an example. In that race, I had twenty minutes to get a cup of coffee and shove something in my mouth and make a call, preferably to my sister: both caffeine and personal connection were essential in order to make it through the rush. I remember waiting for the elevator, hot coffee in one hand and phone in the other, needing to dig into my purse to find keys, tapping my foot compulsively, anxiously waiting for the elevator doors to part.

Beauty before age said a woman's voice behind me. I surveyed my surroundings again, stashed my phone, and took a deep breath. I studied the petite older woman next to me. She smiled coolly and calmly. She was waiting nonchalantly for the elevator; she didn't care if it arrived within the next two minutes or two hours from now. I laughed and said, *No, that's not true, you're beautiful, too.* I asked her age, and she said seventy-eight. She told me she liked being older because she was content. Whatever she had failed to accomplish at this point in her life she would probably never accomplish, and acceptance put her at ease. I thought, "Gosh, I hope I don't wait until I'm seventy-eight to figure out the fine secrets of life." She was another angel advising me to slow down and to rest in the present. I realized overachievers like myself, anxious perfectionists, fight emptiness caused by perceived lack of achievement or accomplishment, filling the void with low self-esteem, depression, loneliness, and the need to control. *God had winked.*

I gave birth via C-section four times, my biggest baby weighing over ten pounds after I was diagnosed with gestational diabetes halfway through my pregnancies. It was controlled through diet, insulin, and exercise. All of our children are two years apart. We moved six weeks after each of my pregnancies, and I had jobs without maternity leave. The stress mountain got higher. We had a baby with colic for four months with no family nearby to help. A feeling of overall lack of support seemed insurmountable. These circumstances were all high risk factors for postpartum mood and anxiety disorders. I experienced postpartum panic and anxiety at varying degrees, beginning around three months after each birth, with varying intensity. I never enjoyed pregnancy or the infancy stage and finally learned to accept I'm just no good with pregnancies or with little babies.

Something helpful to me when a first time mom were weekly calls with my girlfriend Susan in Chicago. We were the first of our friends to have children. I looked forward to our absurdly early PST Saturday morning conversations about parenting, relationships, body changes, and sex. It was a safe, supportive, non-judgmental relationship that helped me to grow as a woman, as a wife, and as a mother. I tried a support group for new moms, but I was trapped within my own internal judgments of perfection, getting caught in a competitive cycle of comparisons and finding the task counterproductive. I know other women find great support in this arena. It's subjective.

On a given day, you may exercise, take your kids to school, go to work, experience road rage on your way home while thinking about which sexy lingerie to wear for your partner, get home, deal with dinner, bath, and homework, lie in bed thinking about that lingerie, have good intentions of having sex, but fall asleep. We feel depleted and irritated and wonder why?

Many women have an ongoing *More, please, I can do it all* Super Woman mentality that's been ingrained in us since we were children. We try our best to do it all and rarely say no. I certainly exemplified this attitude for many years, which resulted in anger, bitterness, and resentment. I found myself drawn to meditation books for women who simply do too much. I was so stressed, however, I found no time to meditate, causing more stress and entertaining thoughts of burning that sexy lingerie.

A large percentage of the population struggle with striving to do too much and with asking for even more responsibility to fulfill some other need. Some may say this is normal, that we all want to strive to be our best and to feel a sense of accomplishment when we reach our goals. Absolutely! It's important, however, to recognize the difference between healthy anxiety which motivates us, and problematic anxiety, which creates stress and can overwhelm us. We could be engaging in wonderful adventures without actual presence in the present moment. I choose to be fully aware, observing and experiencing, tasting and smelling, looking, listening, and touching. I want to stay excited about all life has to offer.

Our second baby cried non-stop for four months. The only hope for peace was if she was bouncing on an exercise ball while we shushed loudly into her ear, or if she was sucking on my breast. She rejected the bottle when I went back to work and refused to eat for twenty-four hours. We simulated an environment similar to the womb, which the pediatrician referred to as creating the fourth trimester. We bought every baby wrap available to keep her tight against our bodies so she could hear our heartbeats. I slept with her on my chest even though the pediatrician said not to. We kept a vacuum running next to her bassinet and sound machines in every room, faux waves crashing on the beach mimicking the sound of rushing amniotic fluid. Walking into our home felt like a black hole you might get sucked into. Nobody wanted to be left alone with this child and the struggle to soothe her, a terrifying development. The doctor warned me that good people can do bad things to their child when they can't get them to stop crying. Put her in a crib where she is safe, continue to check on her, but wear ear plugs and distract yourself with an activity around the house. I wrote, *YOU ARE A GOOD MOM, BABIES CRY* on a butcher paper and taped it to the wall so that I could remind myself I wasn't failing. Taking breaks was the only way to recharge.

It made sense that I was overwhelmed and felt like I was doing something wrong. For any women with a history of mood or anxiety disorders, we are at higher risk for experiencing a form of postpartum depression not to be confused with the classic baby blues which typically subside after two weeks postpartum after the shift in hormones, the symptoms irritability and crying while the woman's body tries to readjust. Even without a history of a mood disorder, women can experience more insidious postpartum depression, using the term very broadly as an umbrella, with anxiety and panic and obsessive-compulsive disorder as a form, with worst cases experiencing psychosis. Researchers aren't exactly sure why, but sleep deprivation seems to be a strong contributor. If symptoms last longer than two weeks, or if thoughts of hurting yourself or your baby arise, then it's important to contact your

OB-GYN, who will link you to a psychiatrist or to someone such as me for psychotherapy. It is not a character defect; *you are not a bad mom.*

After each birth, I had difficulty sleeping, even though I was exhausted. I'd fall asleep for an hour and then wake up in a panic, sweating. My thoughts never stopped racing. I cried frequently for no reason. Starting a married life together in Santa Monica was a blessing by giving us the opportunity to really bond and to lean on one another and to build a solid foundation, my saving grace through our role as parents. I'm so proud of myself for trusting and for listening to Ryan. Being pushed out of our comfort zones over and over again ultimately afforded us a huge boost of confidence and a *We can do anything* attitude. After six years, we finally decided to move back to Chicago, returning with three children, ages four, two, and a newborn. It felt so good to be back in the place I call home. We spent a few weeks getting acclimated, friends and family stopping by religiously. Our third child was amazingly tranquil. With many hands to help, mothering an infant became a reparative experience the third time around. Life seemed to be a little more manageable for the time being—until I went back to work.

I had been teaching a graduate course in conjunction with seeing clients, which meant I was busy, to say the least. I remember the supersonic gliding sound of the speeding El train hitting the tracks. I was reading an article, when out of the blue I had a panic attack. It wasn't my first panic attack, but I hadn't experienced one in many years or one quite as intense. It felt like an elephant was stepping on my chest, and I couldn't catch my breath. It was relentless. The more out of control I felt, the more heightened the panic. Incensed, I tried to push it away, which only increased my alarm. Because I treated panic and anxiety, I knew all of the tools to use. Accept the panic, and try to restructure thoughts. *This will pass, you are absolutely okay, your stop is coming soon.* Nothing worked. It was my first day of class, and so I tried to recover by breathing and by drinking water to refocus my attention, mindful about what was right in front of me. I roughed it through the distribution of the syllabi and hid my internal struggle. It had lasted for hours.

I had not yet chosen a doctor since our recent move, and so I was at a total loss. I felt embarrassed and ashamed, because on paper there was no reason for me to feel this dreadful, or so I thought. We'd just experienced several major life transitions at once, another risk factor. I was quite aware of that fact, but I was elated to be home. I was close to friends and family. I loved my job. My children and our marriage were blessed. I was struggling yet again, however, with postpartum anxiety and panic. The first two times I had PPD symptoms made more sense to me. I'd had my first child in a new environment in California and we had no support and we were financially stressed and my overachieving personality and undying need to be perfect got into the way of my parenting. I was aware that many others had *real* problems. I didn't feel as though my miniscule problems warranted panic attacks or overriding anxiety. I knew how fortunate I was to have a loving husband, a home, a job, a healthy baby. Rationally, I got it; emotionally, not so much.

Women often never report their symptoms, and they go untreated, trying to navigate on their own. The misconception is that postpartum depression is the inability of a woman to bond with her baby or has a desire to kill it. This certainly happens, but it's the far end of the spectrum. The best treatment option is a combination of medication and therapy. I was hard on myself for the type of mother I thought I was supposed to be rather than trying to do my best and accept my limitations. I was juggling many pins in the air, and I wanted them all to be shiny and perfect, no achievable goal.

I learned to ask for help and to accept the help given to me. It truly does take a village to raise a child. No family support in Santa Monica with our first two children presented the necessity to hire babysitters on weekends to get a little reprieve and some time alone. Our mothers gave us the most amazing gift, their time and service, by caring for our children so we could vacation in Mexico. I gave up breastfeeding when I returned to work, because it became too chaotic to pump between sessions. After my first child, I needed to restructure my thoughts about failure. I needed to acknowledge that it wasn't failure if I didn't nurse my baby for a year; that it wasn't failure if I didn't meet certain milestones. What I needed was to measure reachable goals. I needed naps or early bedtime to manage sleep deprivation; even medication was necessary. I needed to eat frequently, even just small snacks every two to three hours when I had no appetite, and I needed to limit my caffeine and alcohol intake—all seemingly simple, basic, daily tasks to manage, although a woman's caretaking of her family and her struggle with body image issues, a result of gaining twenty-five to fifty pounds during pregnancy, throw a wrench into simple. A low libido resulting from nursing increases the clench of that wrench. Returning to work or acclimating to an environmental change while attempting to maintain all relationships can seem a daunting task and, at that point, forget the wrench; you need a bulldozer. KEEP IT SIMPLE!

I took timeouts in the baby glider and held my babies on my chest. It was a natural relaxant, endorphin rush, and serotonin release. My heart rate slowed, and I enjoyed that moment with what was right in front of me. Unfortunately, men lack focus on the difficult transition into parenthood. Most of the focus is on the mother, for obvious reasons. Often, men aren't granted paternity leave. They, too, are sleep- and sex-deprived. Men have told me they feel helpless because they can't soothe their child as quickly as their spouse. It may take longer for them to attach to their baby because Mom meets the majority of the baby's needs. I encourage you to be sensitive to your partner's needs and to keep strong lines of communication.

This Isn't What I Expected: Overcoming Postpartum Depression by Karen Kleiman, MSW LCSW, and Valerie Davis Raskin, MD, is an amazing resource for women to read before birthing their first child. It was a personal resource, and I suggest it to all of my pregnant or postpartum moms. Like many other mental health symptoms, anxiety can be genetic or an environmentally learned behavior and way of thinking. *High Anxiety* isn't just the title of a film; its real. Anxious parents must break the cycle and must model positive behavior for their children in order to prevent a negative cycle of unmanageability. Below are some examples of anxious parents striving for more and wanting more and projecting it onto their children, who then become anxious.

When I was a guidance counselor at a high school, a student strode into my office and asked, *How can I move my class rank up from #2 to #1? What else should I be involved in? I'm the President of the class. I'm the football manager. I'm in all Advanced Placement classes. I'm Student Ambassador . . . what am I missing?* Some of the students disliked some of the activities they participated in but applied themselves, anyway, because isn't that what colleges are looking for? *I need to add more to my resume so they want me.* When I asked the student why #2 wasn't good enough, he said, *It's not the best, and I don't like being criticized.* His need to strive for perfection was a Band-Aid on fear of judgment by others.

Another student entered my office crying when she was denied admittance into Stanford. No other school was good enough for her, which she extrapolated as *Now I'm not good enough, because Stanford didn't want me. Why did I waste all four years of high school working this hard if all I could get into was a University of California branch?* UCSB was a pretty good alternative, in my opinion. She felt the only way she could feel good about herself was through her accomplishments. Her core belief was, *The only way I can get recognition from my family is if I am the best; otherwise, I am a failure.* How about her personal qualities? She was friendly, articulate, made others feel strong and important, and she tried her best. I prefer my children to emphasize the importance of strong personal character and to empathize socially by helping others rather than measure themselves by what they believe they have achieved.

Some adult clients report feeling embarrassed discussing in session some of these overachiever traits, mitigating their problems as *First World problems.* Well, we do live in a First World, which is relative to personal life experiences. Don't shame yourself for wanting more, or deem your problems Not as bad as; re-focus by striving to do and to be your best, just for today.

Living in Los Angeles and Chicago while parenting, I became aware of mothers who are, pardon my language, *Activity Whores.* They push their children to do too much. Structure in a child's life is essential. We know sports and the arts raise self-esteem, but I'm blown away by the scheduling of just a single day before the child has even started school: soccer and swimming in the morning, play date in the afternoon, and gymnastics before dinner, repeating the strict schedule the following day with different activities. My theory is that the rationale is to preserve sanity. Structuring the child's day is what allows parents to structure their day. Pushing to do more . . . and more is a recipe for anxiety, particularly if either or both parents suffer from anxiety. How about allowing your three-year-old to engage in free play? Ask the child what he or she wants to do by offering options exposing them to everything, and follow their lead. I guess that falls under the category of a Montessori approach. No one way is going to create the perfect outcome. There is no script, and there is no perfect scenario. We're going to screw up as parents, and so will our kids. I don't think anybody wakes up in the morning and consciously says, *I'm really looking forward to screwing my child up today.* Laugh a lot, let go a little, and have *fun!*

I want to be a good partner, a good mother, maintaining solid friendships and strong relationships with my siblings. Isn't this what we all want? To feel fulfilled by *having it all?* I've had this conversation with many of my clients. We want it all, but *we want more of it.* We want to be married and have kids by the time we are thirty; otherwise, something is clearly wrong with us—or, we fear that is what others think. If marriage and children are a genuine desire, and you want these things because you're excited about sharing a life with a partner and raising a family, great! Don't worry; you'll find it. If you feel pressure from society or from family but haven't yet found the right person, nothing is wrong with you. Not everyone needs to get married and/or have children. We strive for rewarding jobs, although most people work a miserable job for whatever need it fills. We want friends, money, a good body, and spiritual enrichment. Let's face it, we want it all, and *we want more of it,* and some of us will go to any length to get it. I know I definitely did, and I almost drowned in the whirling cesspool. I was simply unable to keep my head above water no matter how intensely I stroked and flailed.

I am no fortune teller, but chances are that at least one of my four children will experience a mood or anxiety disorder and/or addiction due to genetics. My motherly mission is to model positive behavior and to teach my children healthy coping mechanisms by practicing what I preach. Serendipity set me to working with women struggling with postpartum mood and anxiety disorders. A newly pregnant Los Angeles client, for example, experienced high anxiety about her pregnancy. During her treatment, I guided her through *The Pregnancy and Postpartum Anxiety Workbook,* fortuitously for me: Ryan and I had been planning to move back to Chicago at the time, but I had no job there. In the back of the workbook, there was information about an anxiety clinic sponsored by The University of Illinois at Chicago. I contacted the Director, figuring it was a long shot but took the chance and emailed her. She responded immediately and told me she had relocated to the east coast but connected me to a colleague owning a women's mental health practice specializing in the treatment of postpartum depression, infertility, and loss. I had already learned the hard way about moving to a city without a job and was determined not to sink into that quagmire again. Thus, seven months pregnant myself, I flew to Chicago to interview with several of the providers. I was offered and accepted a job as an independent contractor clinician in a practice with a team of psychiatrists, social workers, and psychologists. I've been incredibly fortunate to have been given the opportunity to collaborate with top OB-GYN's to create a well-rounded holistic treatment approach. I'm honored and privileged to work with hundreds of individuals and couples with a wide range of diagnosis related to career, parenting, relationships, and transitions into motherhood and fatherhood. Our work together is precisely that, a *partnership* in healing and guiding.

Katherine Stone of Postpartum Progress reports that *950,000 women suffer from postpartum mood disorders each year.* Also a professional in the field of women's mental health and the mother of four,

I feel a paramount responsibility to educate women about postpartum depression. An experienced speaker for a large community of pregnant women and mothers, I present an awareness of what to expect and provide resources for treatment. The ideal place for information on support groups, sleep training, and overall mama collaboration is the Bump Club and Beyond, a nationally recognized small business committed to enhancing the experience of parenthood.

Once, before I left for work, my eight year old daughter looked up at me with eyes like an angel and asked what time I would be home. I told her not until bedtime due to a presentation to women becoming moms. She asked why, and I explained that, sometimes after a woman has a baby, she gets sad. *I thought having a baby was a happy time.* This gave me an opportunity to share with her that there are a whole lot of feelings women may have after a baby is born. Some feel overwhelmed, some excited, some in love, some exhausted. *Well, that's weird,* she said. Many of my clients agree. They arrive at my office confused and embarrassed by their emotions. They recognize that having a baby is a true miracle, and maybe it took them years to get pregnant, a baby was all they had ever wanted. *So why do I feel so ashamed?* they ask, their shame the usual reason postpartum sufferers postpone seeking help.

Medication is an option during pregnancy and while nursing. Depending on the severity, it can be prescribed either by your OB-GYN or by a psychiatrist specializing in women's mental health and pregnancy. Many women referred to me start therapy during pregnancy, because they are aware of their higher risk of postpartum depression. This earlier start gives us the opportunity to jump-start with preventative measures such as coping mechanisms and to intercept symptoms early versus waiting until postpartum attacks, because having a baby can unearth unresolved issues we have with our own parents, and having a child is always a major life transition requiring time to adjust and to find *a new normal.* Some women abruptly stop taking their psychotropic medication when they become pregnant due to a fear of harming the baby. The benefits of taking medication during pregnancy for women with a history of mood or anxiety disorders can outway the risks. *Never* make the decision to stop medication on your own. A simple consultation and a review of options with an MD can have a huge positive impact. I've worked with women who opted not to take medication and instead came to weekly cognitive behavioral psychotherapy to manage symptoms. One of my areas of specialty is in treating Obsessive Compulsive Disorder, with intrusive thoughts such as contracting HIV, contamination, or worries that spouses cheat throughout the pregnancy. Psychologically, these women recognize they are having irrational thoughts, but the feeling is intense, and the concrete evidence to negate the thought is never enough. The thoughts and obsessive behaviors typically resolve themselves after delivery, particularly when medication is added, but often the obsessions and compulsions can be transferred to interactions with the baby. Obsessions with baby's sleep, food, weight, and sudden infant death syndrome can become all consuming. *Awareness and talking to someone* about your feelings is the key to a remedy.

I empathize immensely with those navigating the healthcare system. Moving back to Chicago from Santa Monica, Ryan and I were both rebooting our careers. We had no money in the bank, no consistent income, and no health insurance. We applied for a state funded health program so that our children could receive regular care and check ups. We now had an infant needing to be seen frequently by a pediatrician, and I needed medication for my anxiety. We were in over our heads and had mutually concluded that our family felt complete with three children. A non-hormonal IUD seemed to be the best course of action for long term birth control. I called our state-assigned clinic for an appointment, consistently placed on hold for over an hour until I finally left numerous messages never returned. My frustration drove me to take action by driving to the clinic in the belief my presence would be more effective.

I walked into the West Side Chicago clinic quietly, with a nervous stomach and with sweaty hands. I was greeted by a DMV-like, overcrowded waiting room reeking of urine. I dared to look down. The floors were filthy, vending machine trash littering the tables— Oreo wrappers, empty soda cans, and paper napkins strewn about. Mothers watched the sliding glass window impatiently, stressed and tightly wound while their babies screamed, and they desperately tried to soothe them. Aside from the fact that I was just standing there in a quasi dreamlike state, I realized I was a novelty—white, with blonde hair and green eyes.

When I checked in, I was warned of a few hours wait. With no other options, I resigned myself to wait and studied the scene and was mesmerized. I was watching a real life version of the ER on *Grey's Anatomy,* and realized I was desperate but was also confident this debacle, too, would pass. A few hours turned into six, until I was finally summoned to a young woman for a mere consultation. She confirmed that I would be a good candidate for an IUD but that I needed to come back to match the timing with my cycle. I was hoping for a one stop shop and asked if she would prescribe the same medication and dosage I had been on during postpartum with the other kids, when my anxiety and panic had skyrocketed, but she would consent only to a fourteen day supply and referred me to the internist down the hall. There was no appointment available for three weeks, but I scheduled it and returned to the OB-GYN clinic asking for seven more pills tiding me over, which resulted in another hour stint in the waiting room melee.

Three weeks later, despite my appointment, I waited *only* four hours before seeing the internist—better than the eight hour day my previous visit! He prescribed an antidepressant for six months. I knew I'd never go back, deciding I would somehow afford insurance, or I would ditch the meds. I felt such empathy for the other people at the clinic. This care center was the norm of those who spoke no English. When I returned for my IUD insertion, the mayhem remained the same, but my anxiety was qualmed by gratitude for my personal remedy—or so I thought....

Six months later, I realized my period was a week late. Sure enough, I was pregnant. Panic set in. My mind raced with possibilities. Should I have an abortion? I was unsure I could live with myself if I chose that solution. I knew for sure my prenatal care would never be at that West Side clinic! Believing a miscarriage likely, I decided to wait a while. As I discharged from an ER visit on that late Saturday night, however, still unsure of our *plan,* my nurse angel referred me to a clinic associated with the downtown hospital, and I was grateful for care at a more familiar environment, exceptional care, needed for gestational diabetes requiring insulin shots, a special diet, and frequent appointments. I needed a lot of maintenance! I delivered a healthy baby girl with Ryan, Mom, my sister, and my super hero labor and delivery nurse aunt for supporters. *And then I had those tubes triple tied!* . . . Our family was complete, a satisfying package of pure, unconditional love: two boys and two girls.

As an independent contractor and small business owner, we also found our groove. Our life was and has been bountiful, and we can now pay for private insurance for a family of six. One word, astronomical, applies, but I won't get political on you.

Parenting is by far the most daunting job I've ever worked but is also the most rewarding. It is dichotomous and extreme: I go from screaming at my four year old for casing the fridge and pulling out a gallon of chocolate milk and spilling it all over the floor, to laughing and singing while carting her up to the bath! Yes, parenting can feel, seem, and sound psychotic. It starts simply enough, with a drive to the hospital and a birth, the pain forgiven over love and pride for the precious bundle, and a few days later, we take the gift home looking forward to and believing we know how to take care of this tiny person. We have read dozens of books by the time he or she arrives, but we learn suddenly that nothing compares with the experiential learning process, and the learning curve is enormous. Relax, and take your time, because you have your child's entire life for a practice session.

Ryan raises me up. He is to my children the exemplary father I longed for in my own father. Even though we're polar opposites in some ways, we are also very similar, and we understand and support each other, assuring a soothing balance. We are true partners in this world we made together. We've been together for seventeen years, and there were many times our relationship could have crumbled because of my old patterns, my insecurity attaching myself to someone, my need of repair. I wanted to walk away sometimes, and I certainly pushed him away at times, but he stuck by me and always reassured me we'd figure it out, and we'd be okay. The primary reason for our marriage working the way it does is Ryan's sense of security attaching himself to someone else. We are committed to trudging through the tough times, always eased somewhat by open communication even if it's hard to adhere to. That being said, tune-ups are a significant part of reconnecting. There have been times throughout the course of our relationship that we've strengthened it by addressing recurring problems in couples therapy, by spending an overnight at a downtown hotel, or by playing hooky from work after dropping the kids off at school and enjoying the day at home together, uninterrupted. Marriage takes work and rapt, constant attention; we need to make the relationship a priority and nurture it. Weak attempts to grow together as a couple or ignoring issues raise the risk of divorce, infidelity, or insidious resentment.

ONE DAY AT A TIME should be the mantra in a marriage and in daily life. It's simple and helps me see life just for today. Some days, it's one hour at a time. Work/Life Balance continues to be something I try to figure out and to practice daily. My plate is full, but I know genuine joy all day long with family, friends, work, exercise, and random interactions, which make this journey of life more fulfilling. My kids drive me bananas when I'm short-fused, I yell at my spouse and say in the heat of the moment things I sometimes regret, but I am sometimes humbled into admitting my wrongs. I drink too much caffeine and get agitated when life is moving too fast, even when I bring it upon myself. I can't stand making the kids' school lunches or doing laundry. The negative feeling doesn't take away the fact that the task still needs to be completed. I complain about it in my head or aloud, and sometimes I choose to take time to allow appreciation of the moment when I load the soap into the wash, fold the clothes, and stash them away in the drawers. There will come a time my kids will do their own laundry, and I may think, *I miss folding those little socks I could never find the match to.*

My children command my presence with their warmth. The world stops briefly when I interact with them. Holding them on my lap or snuggling is a natural Xanax. All of us are very affectionate. When our sitter picked my daughter up when she first started preschool and my daughter ran into her arms, the teacher said, *I get the sense this is a hugging family.* Close physical contact soothes all of us.

Listening to them read to me as they learn new words, I find myself in awe of their rapid growth, running, biking, and swimming together, enjoying the activities I found great joy in with Al and now with our kids. They are all extremely different, and we could have predicted their personalities as they came into the world. Our firstborn son is an independent, old soul caretaker. Our second child, a daughter, is a natural leader, organized and spiritually aware. The next, a son, is a well-liked, laid back, cool kid despite a hot temper. Our baby daughter who willed her way into this world is a handful but spunky, determined, and hilarious. There is no "one size fits all" way to parent, because all kids are individuals with different personalities and different needs. I enjoy the individuality, and I hope it never changes.

I want to put my oldest daughter's positivity into my pocket and cart it around with me all day. Once, we were driving to join some of her friends at an open gym, and she said, *Mom, when I get excited it feels like I have butterflies in my stomach.* I had a broad smile on my face: she was aware of her mind/body connection. I was pleased to realize positive psychology was transferring to my children. And then there's that precious darling spitting water onto the floor, and when I yelled at her to stop, she looked me straight in the eyes and said, *Mom, don't judge me.* Yep, they can be devils, too. After four rounds of this parenting thing with four little souls, I still don't know what I'm doing, but we figure it out along the way, one day a a time and sometimes, more days than most, one hour at a time—actually, one minute at

a time.

XI

BOOZE

BOOZE & BOYS

The persistent hiss of hairspray, and the powdery chemical cloud of AquaNet lodge in my memory bank, the sound and the smell of freedom. I experienced my first drunk the summer before eighth grade. My best friend Siobhan and I had been invited to a party with her high school cousins, all boys. I was spending the weekend at her house, the perfect set up. I was a regular, more like an extended family member, another daughter—my parents would never suspect a thing. Siobhan had everything an adolescent wanted— music, her own phone line, and a beautiful room fit for a princess; to top it off, she had jewelry and was a makeup and hair pro. I remember the feeling of hooking hoops through my ears, silver drops dangling in a sexy dance. My bangs were expertly curled and cardboard stiff with AquaNet. Siobhan dabbed at my acne, perfectly and smoothly with foundation, before treating me with a Marshall Field's-worthy makeover. I wore my stonewashed Daisy Duke fringed shorts—too short—and a tight tank top—too tight—both brand new from a recent GAP shopping spree, where Al had allowed me to pick out anything I wanted. At the ripe age of twelve and a half, I felt like hot shit, posing and twirling before a mirror confirming that I was, indeed, hot shit. I was almost breathless at the thought of hanging out with the older boys—I simply couldn't wait.

We piled into Siobhan's parents' car for the ride to a Catholic school fair in a closed off parking lot. All the parents were drinking heavily. We spotted her cousins, all of them handsome, charming—and older! Only thirty seconds were required for my crush to land on the eldest boy, a tall, gorgeous, sixteen year old blond in a Notre Dame tank top baring his biceps, and he drove a red Corvette in which the guys whisked us away to a party down the street at the house of someone whose parents were *vamanos* for the weekend. It was a scorcher of an afternoon, and the humidity was ruining my bangs. I kept my arms away from my sides to avoid pit stains on my new tank top. My hot shit persona was starting to melt.

The house was crowded with mostly boys playing quarters and focused on keg stands and beer funneling. Vanilla Ice blasted so loudly, I could hardly hear what the person next to me was saying. I was overstimulated and nervous until someone handed me a cold beer in a blue plastic cup. This marked a milestone in my life. My first drink. I can still taste it and liked the taste of it. One after another went down nicely until I danced in the middle of the room, feeling on top of the world. I identified with all the drinking hype among the bar folk I grew up around, and I agreed: if this was adulthood, sign me up!

My alcohol-fueled high was short-lived. The dancing slowed to crawling into someone's bed. I remember my head pounding and spinning when I awoke in a bed I was unable to remember getting into—an unfamiliar bed. Why was I in it, I wondered, panicking from the confusion. The tall, blonde cousin spread cold cloths on my head, and he and Siobhan told me hours had passed. They fed me to try to sober me up, the ticking clock reminding us we needed to get back to the school parking lot to meet Siobhan's parents. Well, I was no longer drunk but became violently hung over with a headache and nausea. I felt as though I had been hit by a car and wished I had been hit by a car, I was so embarrassed and mad at myself. Shame prompted repeated, abject apologies. That was the last time I was invited out with her cousins.

We drove back to her house with her parents, and because *they* were intoxicated, they never noticed my own inebriation. I slept over that night but went home the next day, determined to downplay my weekend. My lying skills were atrocious, precluding keeping up the ruse the remainder of the weekend, and so I hid in my bedroom. I delayed experimenting with alcohol again until I was in high school. I could never fool Mom, however, always alert to my flirtation with libations because she was at the height of her own drinking; she constantly accused me of being drunk after basketball games and assumed that I was running with a fast crowd. If a good girl was never perceived as being good, what was the point of trying? I may as well do what she was accusing me of doing.

BOOZE & PARTIES

My all girls high school community resided primarily on the North Shore of Chicago. The majority of these sprawling estates had readily accessible alcohol, some of the parents even permitting drinking in their basements. By junior year, I had become a stealth operator. Older friends with fake IDs bought me flasks of Southern Comfort for parties, assuring that I never had to drink from the keg. Straight whiskey had a faster effect and fewer calories. When I drank, which became most weekends, I became a "counter" of the number of drinks I consumed in the hope of trying to manage the intake. I was, in effect, setting up damage control, my rule an odd number of drinks. If we were at a party and someone said, *Let's have one more drink* and it was number six, I made sure I had two more drinks to make it seven. It needed to be either five or seven, never six. It was absurd and compulsive, my delusion of feeling in control. I was convinced if I ended on an even number, something bad would happen, and if something bad did happen, I blamed it on the even number. Clearly, it was the even number's fault I blacked out.

The compulsion prevented enjoying my first drink, because I was already thinking about my third drink. I experimented with different combinations. I tried switching WHAT I was drinking. Maybe if I drank only beer, I wouldn't get too drunk. If so, I could have more beer, if it's light beer, because of the calories. I'd eliminate shots, because the culprit might be the vodka. I'd stick to rum. I never created the perfect formula. I'm sure my fellow partiers thought I was a giant lush. I decided on virtual abstinence, my rationale reducing my drinking to special events. I'll drink only for *this* dance or for *that* football game; then I allowed myself to drink for *a* dance or for *a* football game, assuring many more dances and games. I devised the potential insurance policy of offering to be the designated driver, and I was completely sincere, but after a few weeks dry, the *I'm not as bad as . . .* game crept from my mind, and self-justification induced me to compare myself to just about anybody, and I gave in and persuaded myself that drinking was a right of passage, a stage of development, absolutely normal, that an alcoholic was a daily drinker jobless, homeless, or in jail. I granted myself permission to drink again, and the summer before college, I proudly became a full-fledged, card-carrying member, the veritable club president, in fact. I decided to stop worrying and to start living it up.

I did exactly that.

BOOZE & BIKES

In college, everyone binge drank, gorging and then lying listlessly around the next day in a state of misery before powering up and doing it all over again. I was a prime prospect for such mind-numbing inebriation due to overriding conflict at home, and I binged to stop thinking about the dysfunction. I desperately wanted to be a good student but was disappearing into a web of mixed messages and seductive detours. Unable to find a solid core group I felt comfortable in, I self-isolated. When in a "fuck it" mindset, I chose to go out and really cut loose in old patterns of behavior, and they won. I had my mountain bike with me and rode everywhere, even in the dead, Minnesota winter, saving cab fares, because I would never have gotten into a car with a driver who had been drinking. But I couldn't talk after I got a ticket for Biking Under the Influence. It seemed silly and nonsensical at the time: maybe swerving on patches of ice increased risk of falling? And I had thought I was being responsible and safe by biking. I grounded my bike and myself for a while and took up running again, also providing a ready, plausible excuse when people inquired about my abstinence. My excuse was, *I am trying to be healthy,* satisfying the curious and also meeting my need to explain why I got so drunk, how I got so drunk, or why I was abstaining. I never realized until years later that people never think about us as much as we think they do.

The school year end was nearing, however, and because I was leaving for good, I allowed myself one last hurrah. We drank all day and into the night, which sounds like a bad song but which was really just a bad result. I ended up streaking the quad. I painfully remember the humiliation I felt when I walked into the brightly lit dorms and into the brightly lit elevator at 2 A.M. *naked*. This was no Freudian bad dream but an event even more humiliating in retrospect because the people in the elevator were fully clothed, dead sober, and studying for finals. I snuck around campus the next day with my ashamed face hidden by a blue Cubs baseball cap. I loaded a UHaul truck and drove back to Chicago, never to return.

This time I was determined to clean up my act, finalizing my decision by planning to work. I knew how to do that well. I had been a cocktail waitress at Al's bar to save money for my gap year. Surely, once I moved to California at summer's end, my peers would be a more mature, tame group sharing a common goal of recent grads to change the world, working in diligent commitment providing no time to drink all night. I have the uncanny ability to locate fellow partiers anywhere, however, and I met my new best friend, Kate, who had also moved to California from Chicago. We clicked immediately, just as BK and I had bonded. I can pick my soul sistas out of a large crowd; I have an energy connection.

Kate and I enjoyed over a bottle *or two* of wine many deep beach conversations about our alcoholism. Butterfly Beach comes to mind: we huddled in a blanket in the sand, knees drawn to our chests, rain pattering our heads and riling the surf into crashing waves roiling from the depths like the visceral, emotionally turbulent stories from our pasts, creating an HP moment. I'd found someone else struggling with alcohol, someone else who had never spoken to another about the battle, and an unbreakable bond formed between Kate and me. I'd finally found a kindred spirit who knew no one from back home. I trusted Kate with my secrets and knew I could be vulnerable without being judged.

A burden fell from my shoulders: I had an ally in my war on alcohol abuse. We researched. We read *Drinking: A Love Story* by Caroline Knapp, the story about a highly functioning but alcoholic New York woman. We rationalized: if we didn't drink during the week or during the day, we escaped the black label *alcoholic*. Yes, sirree, both of us were experts at rationalizing and concluded we were free spirits with the spirits, and this year was just an adventure. We could quit later if we wanted to. It was an unbinding choice we made in the delusion of our bondage.

BOOZE & WONDER WOMAN

The Bay to Breakers in San Francisco is a 7.46 mile race from the San Francisco Bay to the Pacific coast. The race is known for participants wearing costumes, some in varying degrees of nudity. We signed up without a second thought and stayed with a friend's brother we'd never met, the normal hospitality for the City Year community. He left the key in his mailbox, and we crashed on his couch after an evening exploring the city and drinking dirty martinis in the Mission district.

The alarm went off at six A.M., and we donned Wonder Woman bathing suits, Afro wigs, and sneakers. We had become our alter egos. While waiting for a taxi, I noticed a plate of brownies on the counter with a sign saying, *Warning! Pot brownies.* I'd never *eaten* marijuana before and didn't particularly like weed, because it made me paranoid. The first time I ever smoked pot was with BK, who had expertly instructed me how to inhale from a bong after one of our Friday nights out in the *Viagra Triangle.* I blew into the bong while listening to her coaching—*pull it up*— which resulted in spilling bong water all over myself. It just wasn't my thing. My stomach screamed for food, and I needed something to kick this hangover, and so I cut a very normal, Duncan Hines-looking, brownie for Kate and myself, and we were on our way.

Before long, I couldn't figure out where that laughing hyena was; where was that raucous noise coming from? Was it an *Animal Kingdom* talk show on the driver's radio? After a few minutes, I realized that I was the hyena, which only made my hyena-steria worse, going from a crazed, wild dog laugh to no noise at all, like that voiceless—barkless— Australian dog, the *basenji,* emitting only tears of laughter drenching my cheeks, and I doubled over to stop my diaphragm from forming a six pack from the intense, laughing workout.

Our cab pulled up to an area where few people were costumed, and, suddenly, I stopped laughing. Now I was hyper-paranoid and refused to get out of the car. Clawing the door handle and digging my sneakers into the rubber floor mat, I refused to budge. In true Kate fashion, she said, *Come on; stop being ridiculous.* She grabbed my hand and pulled me from the cab and dragged me to the start of the race. I heard a gunshot. My whole body heard the gunshot, but I had a slightly delayed reaction. While I processed the gunshot, a group of gay men in skimpy G-strings rushed past us pushing grocery carts with kegs—another HP moment.

We caught up to them and chugged a beer, which killed some pain and enabled the easiest race I'd ever run. Slow and steady was our mantra. We made it to the coast finish line and collapsed on the beach and napped two or three hours. Upon waking, still in my Wonder Woman attire, we cabbed back to Kate's car and knew the way to San Jose. Never missing a beat, we swung through the In-N-Out drive-through for much needed fast food and returned to our service work the next morning to do what we loved most: angelic behavior.

JUST BOOZE

Rampaging laughter, clashing glasses, clinking ice cubes, and the pop and hiss of champagne were the sounds of my lullaby. I had grown up surrounded by a drinking crowd and am unable to recall many times when the venue differed. I was drawn to drinkers and felt very comfortable, and still do, in drinking situations most of the time. Nobody challenged the consequences, and they laughed with me, not at me, when I shared my stories. Vacations and holidays granted universal permission to be over-served. I deserved the ticket, and I always made sure I earned it by playing bartender at parties, also ensuring that other people were getting as plastered as I was so that they failed to notice I was myself three sheets to the wind.

I processed alcoholism similarly to my behavior during my eating disorder, overly consuming, doing something I regretted, blacking out, abstaining forty days of Lent, abstaining during marathon training, cleansing in January as though abstinence were my New Year's resolution. I educated myself with the delusion that if I was intelligent enough, I could dodge the alcoholism bullet.

Even my graduate internship, facilitating Intensive Outpatient groups for people with substance abuse issues, facilitated my growing self-delusion, because I didn't relate to treatment mandated after getting caught drinking or showing up drunk at work or repetitious DUI's or losing my family.

Yep, I was above that fray: thus, my kind of binge drinking, although still in my early twenties, was socially acceptable.

After connecting with Kate over problematic drinking, I risked discovery on numerous occasions by approaching friends and family members and expressing my concerns about drinking and alcoholism, only tenuously, though, taking inventory on others' opinions of the type of people they thought qualified as alcoholic, searching for hard and fast characteristics. They responded like doting old maid aunts with, *You have nothing to worry about—you're not an alcoholic; you're just really hard on yourself.* This crowd included Mom, who'd been sober for twenty years. After one night of binge drinking, I fled to her house crying hysterically about my fear that I was a problem drinker. Like other loving mothers, she tends to minimize some of her childrens' demons, and so she seemed to greet my distress with disbelief. Perhaps it was too painful for her, too frightening, because she felt responsible. Maybe I wasn't yet fully honest with my struggle, either: deep down, I knew I had a problem, but I let myself continue playing roulette.

It was never quite reassuring that some of my closest friends blacked out with me and also took part in risky behavior: nudity, bar top dancing, falling asleep on alien floors, extremely inappropriate remarks to a boss or to coworkers come Happy Hour. In my social world, my binge drinking behavior was normalized; thus, the fact it didn't feel quite right with me was canceled out by the fact it had been considered the norm since I was born into the bar world and was raised in it from age toddler to the restaurant and bar jobs from eighteen to twenty-five for college tuition. All the establishments employing me had a common culture with commonplace late night hours until 5 A.M. In fact, all the local bar keep from various neighborhood taverns met up to decompress from a night of serving drunk people. We were a dysfunctional community who could hardly wait to drink together. Of course, I hated how I felt every afternoon after waking up, my anxiety and worry reaching the roof.

I wondered why colleagues and customers never seemed to beat themselves up like I did myself. I attended my first *meeting* at age twenty after one rough weekend, but I could find no one to relate to, and there was a vast age difference. They told me to *look for the similarities, not the differences.* After three meetings, I decided I was no problem drinker. Once again, I felt atypical of alcoholism. My family and friends were right; I was too hard on myself. I merely needed to cut back. I tried Moderation Management, but who was I kidding: I'm no rule follower, but I would try it, a behavioral change model based not on abstinence like some other programs but rather a behavioral *management* of my alcohol intake. The menu was two drinks total *at one sitting,* alternating each cocktail with a glass of water. Only eight drinks *total* were permitted all week. This technique worked a couple of times, but I kept drinking for ten more years with continuous, outrageous blackouts. I was unable to flip the switch in my brain off once

I started. I never craved alcohol; once I started, however, I couldn't stop.

I racked up points of shame and humiliation. Harry Haroutunian, MD, explains that shame is the feeling that *I am something bad and others know it* and that guilt is the feeling that *I did something bad and I know it.* Shame and humiliation make one feel worthless and inadequate, the antithesis of self-worth. Although shame is a horrible feeling, I am grateful I experienced so much of it, or I would never have been motivated to change my thinking and behavior.

I frequently cringed with self-disappointment and shame the next day for offending someone by something I had said the night before. I felt shame for endangering myself by falling asleep on a curb or by urinating in the street after being out all day and night after running my first marathon. At age twenty-three, I felt shame for *popping a squat* behind a car on Lincoln Avenue and getting arrested for public intoxication. I felt shame for having to go to court to listen to a group of neighborhood activists testify against me, claiming I was a disgrace to their community, resulting in community service on the highway shoulder, spearing garbage. Conversations with others fulfilling their service requirements were actually just questions sessions. What was I there for? I was embarrassed by my white middle class petty crime. I wanted to concoct a cooler story to impress my crime buddies of the day. Eye opening was the experience of sixteen hours among men working community service for drug possession, for carrying weapons, or for domestic violence. What the fuck was I doing there with them? I laughed it off and returned to business as usual. I still wasn't ready to surrender.

One of my last big blackouts was after a Cubs game on August 20, 2011. I went with BK and with both of our sisters. I was proud of myself for giving myself permission to be out all day and to have a good time because, let's face it, there had been a dearth of *fun* lately. Ry was at home with the kids, covering all "child duties." Bottom line, I was off the hook. Day time drinking at Cubs games was typically a headlong disaster for me. But that was back then. I approached the day cautiously, telling myself to *pace your drinks . . . drink water after every beer . . . no shots or hard alcohol; stick to Bud Light . . . one Blue Moon is okay, but . . . you can't drink those like Bud Light or . . . you will end up on your ass.* Do nonalcoholics hear this much inner dialogue? Surely they do; doesn't everybody? *Don't waste the space in your head!* At the start of the day, I had girded myself with my drinking armor, and I felt in control.

It was a balmy rather than a humid summer day, just perfect for baseball. We sunned ourselves, swilling and sipping beer in large paper cups ripping and tearing from condensation. I ate a hot pretzel for lunch, my food quota, and threw back a few shots at bars surrounding Wrigley Field. What had happened to the rules I set that morning? Despite the best intentions of trying to be *Good Kelley,* they flew out the window and blew under the bleachers. I told myself I could handle it. After the fun at the game, I drank Red Bull and vodka. Starting to feel tired or *drunk,* I wanted to stay out, because I needed to wake up! In the past, this ruse was the magic potion for longevity. I called it liquid cocaine but much safer. We drank it in Europe all the time; they served it in pitchers at the bars, so no problem, huh? . . . Well, maybe a small problem, because, this time, there was a different outcome. Houdini came to life. When I got too drunk back in the day, I had a reputation for playing *Houdini* and disappearing. My friends were accustomed to this exit strategy, and when unable to find me, they assumed I was too drunk and had gone home.

It was still light, but the bar was crowded, and I was seeing double and was spitting on the floor, usually a sure sign I was over served. When I hit a wall, I decided to go home. I left the bar alone without telling anyone. Unable to find a cab, I boarded a bus. I had a one hundred dollar bill I was trying to insert into the pay slot. I remember having a conversation with the driver about my displeasure with his inability to give me change, while trying to keep my balance as the bus moved forward. Lights went out.

I woke up to a Latino man rubbing my leg. I looked outside into pitch blackness. Apparently, he had stopped his car in our driveway, and in a moment of total panic, I freaked out. I rummaged in my pocket for money to pay him, until he said that he was no taxi driver. He said he had found me on the side of the road looking like someone in trouble, and he had offered to drive me home. I was in a daze, and I babbled incoherently. I jumped out of the car and ran to my front door, flashing back to the attack a decade earlier, reliving the nightmare. Fortunately, my family were asleep. I crawled into one of the kids' bunkbeds with my clothes still on and woke up in total shock with a nagging sense of dread. I sent out group texts to everyone that I was at the game with to try to fit the pieces together, but everyone was asleep, and nobody responded for hours. I kept repeating the Latino man's words in my head: *I saw you on the side of the road and it looked like you were in trouble.* Which road? Where? Why did I look like I was in trouble? What the fuck happened? Why couldn't I remember?

Pacing the house, mumbling to myself, holding myself, I cried in fear. I was ashamed, pissed at myself, hating myself once again, wanting to start over *again.* I drove myself crazy trying to jog my memory and finally woke Ryan up because of my inability to resolve the unknown. He said he had heard me pull up to the house in a cab. I knew this hadn't been the case, because there hadn't been a cab. I remembered the conversation with the Latino man and was mortified. Another bender. At that moment, I promised to write off drinking. *AGAIN.*

My sister finally called me back at 9 A.M., which felt like days later to me. By that time, I was hysterical, and in a calm voice she said she saw me crossing the street at the bar and presumed I was headed home. She told me to calm down and to quit worrying, because I was safe at home. I phoned my other sister, whom I knew would shoot straight with me. "Kelley, you can't do that shit, you have (at the time) three kids and a husband who need you; that was really dangerous." She was right. I was consumed by anxiety and by remorse, constantly beating myself up replaying the events over and over trying to jumpstart my memory. Eventually, I gave up and tried to pretend it never happened. I detoxed and isolated myself.

Two weeks later, I learned I was pregnant with our fourth child. My initial reaction was fear and pure shock. This was impossible: I'd had the IUD. There is only a 1% failure rate. My thoughts were wild: what if the Latino man in the car had raped me so forcefully, he'd knocked the IUD out of my cervix. What if the pregnancy was the consequence of my drunken behavior?

I called my aunt, a seasoned labor and delivery nurse and an incredible friend since I was little. My entire body was on fire with coursing anxiety while she was on the line, and I asked her the likelihood of my irrational but plausible thinking. The consensus was there was no possible way, but she suggested an emergency room visit. Ryan stayed with the kids, and Mom accompanied me. I was at risk of a possible ectopic pregnancy, or was this hysteria? I knew I needed to get the IUD removed, but the procedure possibly caused miscarriage. I worried that I faced monumental catastrophe.

I left the hospital the next morning with a confirmed pregnancy but a lack of surety the embryo would make it. If it was born, I'd know for sure what happened that night in the Latino man's car if the baby was born of mixed race. If the baby was fully white, I could be sure it was Ryan's. The uncertainty obsessed me. I felt a moment of calm, however, when relief flooded me suddenly after I realized I wouldn't be thinking about alcohol for the next year. Whatever the outcome, it was worth it. I was off the hook.

For a long time thereafter, I wanted to be sober. At the apex of my alcohol abuse, six months after our fourth child was born, I promised myself every morning, *I won't drink tonight.* When four P.M. rolled around, however, my internal dialogue changed to *I have a high tolerance for stress . . . I'm high functioning . . . I never drink during the day,* one of my rules so that I didn't pass out by dinner . . . *I never got a DUI, only a BUI . . . I never lost a job . . . I never went bankrupt—well almost, but it wasn't alcohol related.*

The kids became aware of my drinking. My daughter asked me if she could try some of that *Barbie Girl Margarita* Mommy always drinks. But Mommy always added a couple of extra shots of *Patron; Skinny Girl* wasn't strong enough. I explained to her she couldn't, despite svelte platinum Barbie on the label, because it was just for adults. She said, *Well, I can't wait until I'm an adult so I can drink that.*

When the five o'clock witching hour loomed, I had no resistance. I talked myself into one glass only. I was kidding myself, though, knowing I had never been able to limit myself to just one of most anything. I chose not to drink at some functions because nights are unpredictable, and I feared embarrassing myself or getting into an argument with my boss at a holiday party because I'd surely, brashly ask for a raise. *Are you drinking tonight, Kelley, or not drinking,* my friends always asked. One friend of mine told me I needed to practice drinking more to build tolerance: after a few glasses of wine daily, I wouldn't black out on weekends. I tried that, but it didn't work out well. I stopped drinking wine because it made me feel tired, and I replaced it with *Patron* on the rocks after reading in *People* that it's a stimulant. It worked, producing so much energy, I got everything done that I needed to after putting the kids to bed. Ironically, when I drove to work in the mornings, there was a billboard advertisement for *Patron* right off Ohio Street. I had the uncontrollable urge to vomit at each viewing; it was a *Clockwork Orange* moment reminding me of the insanity: despite many efforts to manage my drinking, I was undermined by a big screen slap in the face advertisement glorifying the poison. The billboard has since changed to a Powerade ad of Derrick Rose saying, *Just a kid from Chicago.* Now I smile when passing it and I think, yeah, me, too.

On January 1, 2013, I got a call from BK, who vowed she was done drinking and was flying home from New York and heading to the Secret Society after hitting rock bottom at a concert with a couple of our friends. She had awakened that morning to their concern. She was out of control and needed help. I thought their advice was a bit drastic, but I supported BK. She called me a couple of times a week relaying her experience, knowing I empathized after sharing through the years my concerns about my own drinking. Each chat reminded me I was struggling with my own addiction to alcohol. We met two weekends in a row for a CrossFit class. I was so hungover I wanted to die. We ordered breakfast, and she eyed me across the table over her tea cup, calmly sipping tea, completely at peace with obvious restored health. I wanted the same. I realized that if I joined her, the decision would have to be final. I could do it; I'm no quitter. Although . . . I couldn't imagine forsaking drinking *forever*. In my rationalizing, she was much worse off than I, and . . . although I was sincerely happy for her, the resolution to quit was not yet for me . . . although I was genuinely elated for her . . .

Bullshit.

She was sober, and I hated it.

I was not happy for her.

I wanted her to fail.

I wanted to slap that peaceful smile off her face.

I wanted to bring her down to my level.

What is it with sober people, who gives a ——!

Some friend I was; I hated myself.

That night, I wondered whether I wanted to live. I despised drinking, but I also couldn't imagine my life without it. I was fucked either way. *I'm done with fighting. I loathe everybody . . . everything . . . I'm overwhelmed . . .*

life is too much . . . I can't hold on . . . I can't do this. I kicked the baseboard hard and did it again. Despair eddied from my aloneness, and I grabbed a couch pillow and buried my face in it for a loud, visceral, scream. I dashed to the fridge, yanked open the door, and dared the chilled Sauvignon Blanc to say *No!* I nabbed it, mumbling something, and poured a large one—and then another. It provided no relief from my stubborn resistance. I grumpily suggested to Ryan we put the kids to bed, and we did, and then we fought. Bitterly. I yelled hateful things. I told him I didn't need him. *I can survive on my own; as a matter of fact, maybe we should get divorced!* He remained calm, as usual, during my temper tantrum, his silence infuriating me. I grabbed my purse, stuffed it with a few Coors Lights, and left without another word. I needed a smoke—several of them— and stomped to my 7-Eleven at the end of the block. I swayed back and forth while rummaging through my purse for money to buy a pack of cigarettes. There's quite a crowd in the evening at 7-Eleven, and they stared at me while I counted quarters and nickels and stacked them on the counter. I left the store with a smoker's sense of relief and roamed the alleys of Oak Park, no particular destination in mind. Cool, fresh evening air rotated with the cigarette smoke, another frustrating dichotomy in my lifestyle, and I popped a beer while still cradling a cigarette. Suddenly, I felt pathetic . . . and I cried. *How was I going to raise four kids?* I recalled Al saying, *I couldn't raise five kids drunk; I don't know how anyone could do it sober.* I stood entranced in self-disgust: *I'm a terrible mom. I'm not domestic. I'm a liar. I hate arts and crafts. I can't cook. I never imagined being a parent would be this difficult. It's too much; I can't do it, because somebody always needs something.* How could I take care of anyone else if I was unable to take care of myself? I lit another smoke and chugged beer, still trying to shut out the imagery: my childhood, booze, food, booze, Ryan, children, booze, BK, booze, no more BK drinking with me . . . I was utterly alone; I had only *myself* . . . My back slid down a stucco wall and landed beside a garbage can in the alley. I closed my eyes to still the spinning. I dared to open my eyes, only to see black night in my alley and to hear only dogs barking like night watchmen croaking, "All is *not* well..." . . . Nope, nothing was well with alley cat Kelley. I prayed nobody would come walking down my alley. The embarrassing prospect of discovery rebooted me: *Kelley, get your fucking shit together.* I dug into my purse and found some gum, popped a plug into my mouth, and slowly started to get up, the wall bracing me, the garbage can my guide, gaping without a lid as though inviting me first of all to stash into it all the mismanagement trash in my life, to empty *myself* . . . I realized I must make a decision, right now—but not quite yet, I rationalized stubbornly. I paced behind a neighbor's house, contemplating knocking on the door. They had invited us over earlier that day to watch basketball; I knew *they'd* be partying. My phone was dead, and so I just showed up. *Hey, I figured you guys would be watching the game; can I come hang out?* Much to my surprise, there was no partying, only a couple of families gathered in front of a tv, and nobody was drinking. They ushered me in. One of the moms poured me a glass of wine, and *we* chatted, although *I* slurred. I leaned on the counter while everyone else watched the game. Hours had passed since I'd "left" home. I heard a knock at the door. There stood Ryan asking if anyone had seen me. He thought that I had gone missing and was about to call the police. I laughed it off too loudly and said I was just hanging out and would be home soon, that I couldn't leave unfinished wine in my glass. I downed the last sip, thanked the neighbors for their hospitality, and went home. Ryan was irate, telling me how worried he was and how "I can't do this shit." I downplayed every word until he went to bed. I raided the fridge for a beer and took it to the garage, collapsing again, this time on the cool cement floor, inhaling the gasoline, thinking harmful things. I was unsure how I would survive living alone or as a mother and wife. I loved BK, but I also hated her for my sudden upheaval. I hated myself for wanting to drag her down, for resenting her success, her *happiness*. I curled into a ball on the oil stains and glanced around at our belongings, bikes, and boxes . . . at our lives. They were worth it; *I was worth it.* I knew what I had to do. I opened the automatic garage door and walked around outside for deep breaths of crisply cool fresh air, realizing, *Maybe I can start over, be born again; maybe I can do this!* I studied the stars and prayed for strength to make right choices, for strength to help me find *myself* again . . . because I was gone. At that moment, I saw myself and admitted I disliked what I had done to myself; at that moment, I snapped the hell out of it, went back inside, locked the doors, and crawled up two flights of off-white carpeted stairs to our bedroom and slept on the floor at the foot of of our bed.

I woke up the next morning in a heart-thumping panic when I remembered the conflict I had caused between Ryan and me. I wanted desperately to erase it all, to take it all back, but I couldn't. I avoided him and the kids and snuck out to meet BK again for our previously scheduled CrossFit class, feeling like death, my penance for heavy drinking. Nevertheless, sweating it out always pressed the reset button. When we returned to our cars in the pouring rain, she told me again how much better her life was without alcohol. I responded with a few moments of awkward, pregnant silence producing from her silent understanding I could see in her eyes, the omniscient eyes of a friend, which made me start to cry. I felt relieved by relenting with details of the pain and distress of my drinking. I had transitioned from binge drinking to daily drinking in order to cope. It was controlling me. She asked if I would like to go to a meeting with her, and my automatic response was, I can't; *I have three bottles of wine in the fridge I have to finish first.* She suggested I pour the wine down the drain, pray about the problem, and attend a women's meeting with her on Wednesday. I knew nothing else to do but heed her suggestion. I was unable to quit on my own, I realized. The disease of alcoholism was progressing in my life and usually hits a woman harder and faster, the pro in me knew. The pregnancy and birth of our four children had saved my life by postponing the progression with intermittent four years of sobriety required for a healthy baby. BK had set the example, and after twenty years of friendship and lots of outrageous, fun, drinking memories, we decided on a joint trek to change our lives. I believe one reason she was put into my life was to pass this miracle on to me. *God had winked at me again.*

I was emotionally and spiritually bankrupt. When I stopped drinking, I read a book I referred to earlier, *Being Sober: A Step by Step Guide To Getting Through and Living in Recovery* by Harry Haroutunian, MD. "The disease of alcoholism and addiction is 60 percent genetic; the other 40 percent is environmental." Based on this theory, I am 200% likely to become an alcoholic.

The choice to quit drinking had a huge initial impact on my marriage. Ryan and I had loved to drink together. I was terrified my marriage would end just like my parents'. We were now two totally different people in a totally different relationship, one sober partner and one nonalcoholic drinking partner, a red flag for failure, according to Al and Fluff's experience. I came home from my class with BK on Sunday, March 10, 2013 and told Ryan, *I am going to a meeting with BK this week, because I have a problem with alcohol.* He was at first unmoved: *Everything is extreme with you. Can't you just try to have a few drinks at a time and stop doing crazy shit?* I told him

I knew I could not. I'd tried for decades. Thankfully, Ryan, as usual, supported my decision. The first three months were absolute hell for us due to changes necessary for me to adjust physically and emotionally to a life without alcohol: no longer going out to our favorite stomping grounds, removing alcohol from the house, and participating in a new world he was no part of. I attended meetings and talked on the phone with other recovering alcoholics. I resumed individual therapy, got back on meds for anxiety and panic, and we attended couples counseling. He picked up my slack at home while I juggled work, family, and navigating my way to sobriety. We missed the *good times* drinking together, because, even though they were unpredictable, my drinking days weren't *all bad*. Ryan never complained, however; he trusted me, and I loved him for his faith in me.

If I start drinking, I relinquish self-control; thus, I am powerless over alcohol. There were plenty of times I drank without incident, and I never drank before four, but whether I drank once a week or once a month or had three drinks or seven, I never liked who I became when I drank. I am a grateful recovering alcoholic. The kids know I have an *allergy* to alcohol, and if I drink I don't act right which is why I abstain. Four years later, some people in my life are surprised that I still go to meetings, but I need the support of the testimonials of those who won the fight for sobriety, and I cherish their support. We reinforce each other every day with literature, uplifting spiritual support, and life experiences, in a camaraderie of emotional riches because we all recognize that addiction doesn't discriminate. We're all different ages, races, sexes, with different occupations, yet we have something in common: an equalizing, powerful program. We discuss managing stress and relationships and how to be the best parents we can be. Ryan appreciates that connecting with other recovering alcoholics is a positive mood shifter for me, my new foundation, in fact—when my recovery is my first priority, customary values seem to fall into their proper places. When I started attending meetings regularly, I saw people from my community—my son's baseball coach, other moms from my children's school, an old professor, my parish priest. At first, that old, familiar *shame* snuck up on me, and I was nervous and embarrassed, but then I recognized we were all there for the same reason. I see fellow alcoholics at gymnastics pick up, at the community pool, in the grocery store, and at the health club. Shame is supplanted by comfort in knowing these friends are my little angels cast throughout my day to remind me that I have chosen the correct course of action.

Forty five days sober, I flew to DC for the wedding of Christie, my companion in Spain. She asked me to be a Eucharistic Minister at the Mass and distribute communion. I was insecure and fearful about abstinence of alcohol at the wedding because of how raw and exposed I felt. I had my sober buddy BK with me, and so I was not worried that I would drink, but I just didn't want to feel uncomfortable. I stood at the altar with the priest, assuming I would be responsible for the body of Christ, the host. When one of the Eucharistic Ministers walked over to me with a chalice of wine, I froze and whispered, "No, thank you," the whole congregation silently studying those of us manning the altar. The minister failed to hear me and motioned for me to take the glass of wine. Profusely perspiring, I said, *I can't,* not my first or last awkward moment in my new Age of Sobriety. I knew I'd be off to the races if I had a sip of alcohol, and I was determined not to allow the start of a relapse at church. I have been to other churches where grape juice represents the blood of Christ, and I consider that more inclusive for children and for alcoholics.

Six months after I got sober, my youngest brother bought my sister and me tickets to the Pink concert. I'd never before been sober at a concert, and I feared temptation or boredom, worries belied, however, by the fact that I had a wonderful time—*I loved it.* I realized I'd go home after the concert without any negative consequences, without ending up on a sidewalk or on a bar floor and that I'd remember every highlight, *every detail,* the Diet Coke and the clear, unclouded view from great seats. Pink flew like Peter Pan down from the ceiling, singing, *Sober. I'm safe up high, nothing can touch me, but why do I feel this party's over? No pain inside, you're like perfection, but how do I feel this good sober?* Tears streamed down my face. My sister reached over and grabbed my hand in silent understanding. Neither of us needed to say a thing; I was unable to, anyway: I was speechless. God had winked again.

A year into sobriety, Kate saw something in me that was different. She asked me how my meetings and the program were going, having noticed a huge change in me: a serenity, a sense of calm, she had never seen. She should know: she had witnessed my roller coaster ride with alcohol for fifteen years. She said my success inspired her, and she had decided to try this sobriety drive, sandwiching me between BK and Kate in the sequence of our decisions to grab hold of the tailgate of the rolling sobriety wagon and to crawl aboard, each uplifting and supporting the others in deep empathy with each personal struggle in the common goal of all to live sober. I had felt God in the mountains and among the poor and during the marathons, experiences I thought were the only ways to assimilate God. Now I see God in the *serene, sober stillness in myself,* choosing today an infilling of trust in God and a resolve to stay on my side of the street spiritually by honestly evaluating my character and by willingly acknowledging my faults, and by compassionately helping others. I let myself feel everything now, and although the feelings are often discomfiting, I no longer numb any of my feelings with alcohol.

According to The National Institute of Health, "5.3 million women in the United States drink in a way that threatens health." Since sobriety, it has been remarkable how many women with substance abuse issues are serendipitously on my caseload. Sometimes, I wonder if some of my life struggles were serendipitous, too, because they sent me a calling card to help others by teaching hard lessons I had learned through tremendous pain, experiences that all the while had been worth it. I was worth it, and these women would be, too. Serendipity?

God had winked.

XII

MY STRENGTH

MONTANA

Before I was at the height of my eating disorder, I participated in an Outward Bound trip for fourteen days in Montana. I met eleven guys and girls at the airport from all over the United States. We hiked and backpacked twelve hours a day, sang together along the trails, and philosophized. We cooked our food at the campsite, carried bottles of water from streams, and we rock climbed, always together. One day, I participated in a solo wilderness expedition for twenty four hours with no food and with only a tarp for my spread under the stars; those same stars I still study and long for. I sat by the river, transfixed by the cool, clear, clean water gliding, sometimes tumbling, over the rocks, my open journal poised in my lap. I was alone at last and serene with no current concerns about fitting in; I felt that I could be *myself* . . .

The return from freedom and serenity to "Alville" was rough. Invigorated and excited about telling him about my trip, he was the same old snide sour puss, remarking, as though eager to stab my pretty bubble with an ice pick from the bar, *So basically, it was a bunch of rich kids sitting on the top of a mountain talking about their idiotic problems.* Fortunately, the afterglow of the journey lingered, and I clung to it for years afterward, despite Dad.

AIDS RIDE

When I worked at the AIDS residence, I became passionate about the cause. The summer before I left for college, I had heard about The AIDS Ride from Minneapolis to Chicago, which lasted six days and for four hundred and sixty-five miles. A high school teacher of mine told me she would be riding. When I inquired about joining, someone archly informed me that I would be physically unable to complete it, nor would I be able to raise the thousands of dollars for the cause required to ride. There is no better motivation than proving wrong someone who insulted you; I was up for the challenge. I trained, shipped my bike to Minnesota, and flew there ready to ride, knowing no one there but chancing a meeting with a woman who worked at one of Al's restaurants. At least I had someone to share a tent with.

God winked.

Hundreds of people came together from all walks of life to rally for this cause. We rode hard and strong. By the last day, while traveling through Rogers Park, I was depleted physically and mentally. I constantly visualized the finish line to carry me through to the end. *Breathe. One pedal stroke at a time. Almost there.* We rounded Lakeshore Drive on a surprisingly tranquil July day, the lake shimmering on our left. People were lined up for miles at route's end, including my family and friends, in an awesome show of unity, as we rode through Grant Park to Buckingham Fountain, my personal ride in honor of two friends from the AIDS residence who attended my high school graduation that year. My heart was full of love! And I had learned to run for my life—for my own health, that is . . . and I became a marathon runner . . .

TEAM IN TRAINING/THE LEUKEMIA & LYMPHOMA SOCIETY

Running was an activity to clear my head and to keep me out of trouble. I ran around the reservoir at school in Minnesota and eventually started increasing my time and miles. My goal was to run a marathon. My experience with marathon running was life changing by challenging me to become healthy and disciplined, physically and mentally. Running was therapeutic, the pulsing endorphins flushing poisons and providing clarity inviting cool objectivity to move in, and I loved nothing more than feeling my body get stronger—strength through training versus the horrible relationship I had experienced with exercise at the height of my eating disorder. I decided to run a few races a year for many years. After I qualified for and ran the Boston marathon I spread my joy of marathon running and became a coach through The Leukemia and Lymphoma Society Team in Training. There were veteran runners in this program as well as first time runners. Every Saturday, we met on the lakefront for long runs while training for The Chicago and Rome marathons. We did speed workouts at a track during the week, and everyone was required to raise a significant amount of money for the cause. It's incredible what our bodies can do when we put our minds to it; how contagious the endeavor can also be!

TRIATHLONS

I gained twenty pounds after I was sexually assaulted. I stopped working out altogether and ate whatever I wanted and whenever I wanted for a year because I didn't want anyone finding me attractive, the problem my own disdain of my body's lack of conditioning and a priority on first healing emotionally. Eventually, I realized I would need to heal physically, too. I signed up for the Chicago Triathlon and Steelhead ½ Ironman in

Michigan slated for the following year. I wanted to get back into shape to prove to *myself* that my body was no longer damaged. I have no clue how I completed the ½ Ironman, an out of body experience lasting six hours. My sister had driven me there the night before, and she rose with me at five A.M. to start the race. As we walked out the hotel door, she realized she had forgotten her running shoes and wore only flip-flops, although she planned on running the last six miles with me. She pooh-poohed my worry, said she would figure something out and would see me along the course. The route lacked spectators, and I had to dig deep into my resolve to stay motivated and not give up. The majority of the race was me alone, with my thoughts, the only music the pulsing throb in my veins and my elevated breathing. I finally saw my sister at a distance cheering me on when I ran from the lake to my bike, but I never saw her again until I hit Mile Seven of the run. She waited for me on the sidelines in a pair of shoes one size too big, which she had borrowed from a woman she met along the course. Her spiritual support carried me to the finish line. I completed the 1/2 Ironman. I fell exhausted to my knees, kissed the ground, and cried tears of joy.

HOT YOGA

I've slowed down; thus, the intensity of my workouts has decreased. I am a retired endurance sport participant. It's an accomplishment now if I can squeeze in a thirty minute outdoor run or a spin class. For exercise now, I love hot yoga, which includes sequences of postures and breathing exercise performed at a room temperature of one hundred degrees, all moves designed to systematically work every part of the body. The class is an exercise practicing presence of mind and meditation.

BEING STRONG

I haven't forsaken running, however. BK and I have a pact to run a Hawaiian marathon for our fortieth birthdays, and if any of my children ever want me to run a marathon with them, I'll be honored to oblige, although, by then, I may have to run slowly, jog, walk, skip, or hop or merely enjoy the scenery. Currently, however, instead of constantly beating myself up to go faster or harder, I take advantage of the relaxing, rejuvenating reasons to run . . . *because I am no longer my worst enemy.*

XIII

MY CLIENTS

You better not tell anyone, not even God, a client says. I listen, watching body language so reminiscent of my own anxieties since childhood: eyes downcast, avoiding contact, heart pounding, breathing labored, and my eyebrows suddenly shooting up in defensive challenge. I picked nervously at the sides of my thumbs, and I stained the armpits of my shirt with sweat rings in my soaring anxiety. This reaction still occurs in adulthood. If standing, my legs crisscross, and my thigh muscles tighten; simultaneously, toes curl upward, transferring pressure to the heels. If abused or verbally insulted, my abdomen stabs me with aching jabs of intense rage. I internalize fight mode, my fists balling, and my voice shrills with objection . . . When I'm with a client, I know empathy, and even fight to hold back tears . . .

Thus, when in session with my clients, my eyes knowingly scan their bodies to assess body language and verbal language in order to conceptualize their experience. And then slowly we lock eyes—intimate, soul-searching, eye contact capturing vulnerability and signaling surrender. If a patient avoids eye contact, we discuss why and what might be going on. Typically, shame, fear, or embarrassment obstruct the process. I relax my facial muscles so the client perceives neutrality and relaxes. I sip either coffee or water throughout the session, which helps me stay focused. Sometimes, I cross my hands in my lap. I am at my calmest in mind and body when I am in session. For eight forty-five minute sessions a day, I need only to focus on what is right in front of me vis-a-vis my multitasking outside the office with my four children. When I get emotionally close to a patient's struggle because it reminds me of something from my own life, I consciously use a mantra of "one foot in/one foot out" to gauge countertransference or over identification with my patient. Laughter or a smile often help the patient relax, because I seem more human. Surely my eyes tell them, *I have immense empathy for what you are going through* . . . your experience reminds me so much of mine; choosing me to help you seems so . . . *serendipitous* . . .

I help clients achieve measurable, tangible results with a solution-focused, strengths-based, and cognitive behavioral approach. I treat men, women, graduate students, Chief Executives, lawyers, doctors, couples, moms, dads, and individuals divorcing, ages eighteen through eighty-five. My areas of specialty are mood and anxiety disorders, trauma, addictions, sexual intimacy, and life transitions. This intense career chose me, and I couldn't be more grateful. I wish one prerequisite in life for everyone was a year of psychotherapy. We'd become more self aware—and empathic. The commitment to the process is an investment you make in *yourself.*

Some of the work I do partnering with my clients is rewiring automatic negative thoughts and core beliefs. Client Caitlin arrives at 7 A.M. to accommodate her dual, busy schedule of mom and executive. She takes a deep breath and stands gazing out the floor-to- ceiling window overlooking Michigan Avenue while I pour her coffee. We meet in the center of the room with a lilac candle burning and assume our positions, she on the couch and I in my gray cushioned, swivel chair. I proffer her coffee. She begins with, *It's been a long week, and I'm so glad to see you. This is my happy place.* She kicks off her shoes and tucks her feet underneath herself on the couch, and she sips from the white, ceramic shell mug. She says her anxiety has gotten out of control while trying to manage her busy life and a conflict with her husband. Caitlin has been seeing me for several years and has come to acknowledge she longs for male attention, particularly when she drinks, often regretting her behavior. Through the course of her life, she has been raped several times and blames herself for not stopping it, because she wanted to avoid conflict by just getting it over with. She's a perfectionist and an overachiever; she's recovered from an eating disorder and is a child of divorce. Sound familiar?

There are some clients I have a deeper connection to. I call them "the serendipitous ones." Caitlin is one of them. We've had similar life experiences.

I see a lot of my past self in her struggles, similarities producing deep empathy for her. I listen, and I challenge. She has tried to manage and control her drinking for the past year with moderation therapy: staying aware of the number of drinks per day, chugging only beer. The regimen has not worked for her: she reveals that everyone in her life drinks, her job has a drinking culture, and her family are drinkers. She couldn't imagine a life without alcohol: *It would be so boring.* I take a risk after years of working with her by disclosing that I don't drink. Her eyes well up with tears. She reported a sense of relief in knowing that someone else has struggled with substance abuse who didn't appear to be an *alcoholic.* She asked how I stayed sober, and I shared my experience with *The Secret Society* after decades of trying to manage and control my drinking myself. The following week, she arrived for her session and confessed that she had gone to a meeting; we processed her experience. She continues to drink and continues to experience drinking-induced remorse, but this is her process. My hope for her is to find peace with whatever decision she ultimately makes . . .

. . . Client Kevin sits with legs crossed, khaki trousers raised like highwaters to reveal striped socks of purple, pink, and blue. *Thank you for squeezing me in,* he says, eyes misty; *I have something to discuss specifically today that I have been withholding for some time.* Several glistening tears appear while I wait for him to continue, and the water droplets increase in intensity like the sudden dark clouds obscuring the usual bar of sunlight that usually creases my office

like a ramrod rainbow. I study the gray billows when Kevin does. I am silent.
This is his moment to think for himself and to reveal or not to reveal, but
I suspect the likelihood of a forthcoming bomb about his drinking. *As you
know, we've been discussing my occasionally excessive drinking. Well, it has become
more than occasional; in fact, I've become preoccupied with it . . . to the point that I
wake up and look forward to lunch when I can order several beers with my burger
or steak. Actually, that's a lie. I don't even eat lunch anymore—I just drink.* Like
many of my clients, Kevin continues with a meandering ramble through the
amalgam of reasons for his growing habit: stress, financial worries, a difficult
childhood. While he speaks, I hold my head so that my chin and neck form
a nearly ninety degree angle, allowing me to look dead-on into his green
eyes. I, too, fight tears while I listen. I feel like the wind has been knocked
out of me, the story is so intimately familiar. I feel proud of him for having
the courage to take the first step in finally recognizing his struggle with
alcohol after years of our working together. I also feel suddenly vulnerable,
his addiction hitting close to home, although Kevin doesn't know my mind
had quickly flashed back to my own struggle as a binge drinker and to the
painful difficulty of finally admitting it was time to stop.

I regain focus with a conscious decision to artfully hold space for his
feelings and to shift mine. I nod to express understanding, *empathy*. Folding
my hands in my lap, I say gently, Kevin, you are so brave. I ask him to tell
me more and reassure him there is no judgment. Tears dart down his face.

He grabs the box of Kleenex, dabbing desperately to staunch the flow. I tell him *it is okay to let go.*

Kevin begins to provide more specifics about his story—for example, that he is unable to sleep at night unless he passes out from drinking. Massive bouts of anxiety ensue next morning when he tries to pull himself together to charge through his sixteen hour, high-stress, high-powered attorney day. Several days earlier, he had told his wife he was working late but had stayed downtown to spend the evening with a high class call girl at The Ritz. He hangs his head like Charlie Brown and mutters, *I'm so embarrassed and ashamed. This isn't the type of father I want to be. I promised myself I wouldn't make the same mistakes my father did and here I am repeating the fucking cycle.* His voice begins to rise in anger, and he tosses his head in disbelief. *How did I get here?* . . .

I partner with clients to take risks by expressing themselves in relationships. My single clients in the dating world often wander in wondering what they did wrong when they had thought a date went well but had never received any follow-up. *Why didn't he call me back? Was it something I said?* My clients are surprised by my response: *Why don't you call him and ask? What do you have to lose?* When they try to break things off with someone they are no longer interested in and ask, What should I do? . . . I suggest they tell the truth and tell them they are not seeing a progression in the relationship. If only we were more honest with each other, we wouldn't be left guessing another's moods or behaviors. We would feel less anxious, because so much of anxiety in relationships are based on perceptions of another person's words and actions—and are actually just judgments in our own heads, usually faulty. Simply *be honest* with the other person . . . I ask my clients to *be honest with me* . . .

Each morning in my office, I prepare to absorb the energy of that day's roster of clientele by lighting a candle and by reading a motivational quote and sitting quietly thereafter. Between sessions, I stare out the window in silent prayer. I snack for energy firing up the brain. Writing up my notes is a personal therapy. At day's end, I snuff the candle and reboot my physical energy with an aggressive session on my stationary spin bike, and I pump until purging that day's emotions. I sometimes strike a few yoga poses on my mat, which stays put in my office, or I prop myself against the wall on my meditation pillow and let my eyes swim in the lake. And I breathe, deeply, until I calm myself again. When the notion of home beckons, I jump into my sexy minivan I call *Foxy Lady,* and blast music, windows down, while the Windy City buffets my face. I sing, jamming hard core gangsta' rap at the top of my lungs, hand gestures included, releasing my well of joy. Before I walk into the house, I coach myself with a pep talk about my most important job, *my family.* All the kids are at ages needing and wanting lots of attention. I always try to make sure I reserve enough energy for them and for Ryan, too. I don't always succeed, but that's okay; I'm okay not being perfect.

XIV

MYSELF

Most of my life, I've heard, *Things were never THAT bad . . . You were never ACTUALLY sexually abused; he just touched you inappropriately. It wasn't rape. He didn't penetrate you, and you got away. Stop feeling sorry for yourself . . . You didn't really have an eating disorder; it's not like you got below ninety pounds or needed to be hospitalized. Don't all girls and women have body image issues? . . . You didn't have postpartum depression; it's not like you ever wanted to kill your babies . . . You're definitely not an alcoholic. If you are, then I am. It's not like you drank everyday. Those meetings are for old men who smoke cigarettes and end up in jail . . . You seem fine to me . . .*

I needed someone to hold me and to tell me I would get better. I needed somebody listening, paying attention, and checking on me to ask how I was doing. People are so afraid to ask. They dislike upsetting someone or merely want to avoid discomfiting inquiry. True compassion can be accompanied by silence—by just being there, listening, with knowing eyes showing concern for someone else. We never have to be problem solvers; there is never always a solution to *every* problem, anyway.

Because I believed at an early age that I had no concerned, judicious person to consult and to share my dark secrets with, I had started a journal when I was twelve years old. Mom had always encouraged us kids to record our thoughts and feelings, anyway, and modeled the positive behavior by journaling every morning before we woke up. She sat on the light green suede couch in the living room, pen and journal in hand, listening to music on her bright yellow Walkman while sipping hot coffee, cherishing a busy mother's quiet time.

My journals came in handy later on, because the desire to write a book had always been a long-term goal of mine. I was unsure of the process and had not yet chosen a topic. One ordinary Saturday morning, I decided to rummage through some old boxes in the basement. I riffled through trips down Memory Lane, all the while dancing and singing to Florence and the Machine's *Shake it Out* on repeat, sloshing a large mug of piping hot Joe, occasionally managing between moves to guzzle the black liquid, simultaneously keeping beat with the music by tossing staccato laundry items into the washing machine. *And it's hard to dance with the devil on your back, so shake it out. I like to keep my issues strong, but it's always darkest before the dawn.* Laundry loaded, I tossed some sweater-filled boxes around and suddenly espied nearly twenty journals, my journals since early adolescence, forgotten in adulthood, reflecting feelings, thoughts, anxieties, experiences, and lifestyle themes. Stumbling upon this cache was another example of serendipity and was the birth of the ideation of *My Self* and of my business, SERENDIPITOUS PSYCHOTHERAPY, LLC.

I present to you . . . ME . . . *myself* . . . withholding nothing, hiding nothing, ashamed of nothing. I stand naked before you fully sober in body, mind, and spirit. I am eager to share my gratitude for my well-being in hope of inspiring others to become *the best* version of themselves. The testimonials and stories of others helped me heal; *my* storytelling *continues* to help me heal by sharing my experiences, newfound strength, and hope for the future. I'm a visual and auditory learner; I must see and hear in order to trust and therefore could never have succeeded alone. My hope is for you, too, to find and to be your authentic self. Own your story, because I have learned we all have a magnificent one to tell. I'm not suggesting you should tell the world your story for others, as I am doing, but *do it for yourself.* Baring yourself is incredibly inhibiting, yet also liberating, providing a triumphant rush of adrenaline, the free, *natural,* high that I call *joy.* Write your story in its entirety. Leave nothing out. Choose one person you fully trust to share it with. Present your gift to *yourself.*

I continue to be a work in progress. The past four years, I have been predictable, accessible, consistent, true to my word, soul searching, and eager to help others. I believe in the power of a balanced life rather than a neurotic one, and my goal is striving to make life happier for my daily contacts while inculcating *my life* with the fullest capacity for joy. My Catholic education and the overriding example of selflessness, Mother Teresa, mentored me into a deep, abiding sense of social justice spurring me onward to serve others benevolently.

I write this book for you. My volume of words documents my earnest desire for you to heal, to learn self-love and self-appreciation, and to dump your load of shame. Drug and alcohol addiction, sexual trauma, eating disorders, and postpartum depression are shame-inducing, insidiously secretive illnesses, and my job is a sense of responsibility to heal their survivors. In these pages, I hope you find strength and shame no more. The mountain CAN be moved! Obviously, there are occasional days in the valley of doubt and insecurity, but I am too strong to surrender, because I finally learned to love *myself*. Please learn to love yourself, too. It's a rough hike, but take one step at a time, one day at a time, and when you reach the mountaintop and touch other victorious stars, you, too, will soar with heavenly joy.

GOOD ENOUGH

The last few years have been BIG for us. We bought a house and decided to settle in the diverse community of South Oak Park, just west of downtown Chicago, to raise our family. We opened my practice, Kelley Kitley SERENDIPITOUS PSYCHOTHERAPY, LLC, in my dream building on Michigan Avenue in downtown Chicago. I've been traveling

nationally and speaking on women's mental health issues. In the last year, my

expertise has been featured in over one hundred publications such as *The*

Chicago Tribune, Chicago Parent Magazine, The Wall Street Journal, Huffington

Post, Self, Shape, and on *Fox News.* I've been interviewed on podcasts, tv, and

radio shows, and then I decided to submit *My Self* for publication. Ryan

achieved some phenomenal goals too, most notably booking two shows as

an actor at The Goodman Theatre in Chicago—a twenty year old dream

come true! We're on the same success page together at last! The kids are in

school and are thriving. We are blessed.

FAMILY

My relationship with my brothers and sisters is strong, and we are

close. They are my soulmates, and together we have processed much of our

family dynamic to make sense of the dysfunction so that we can relinquish

residual anger. The relationship with my sisters is like no other relationship

I've ever experienced. They are my best friends, as I imagined sisters to be,

and we've often parented each other and each other's children. My young-

est brother manages Al's bar and seems to enjoy the fast-paced lifestyle and

the connection he has to Al that it provides. All of us worked at the bar for several years in our twenties and bonded more readily with him because we were on his turf.

The brother closest in age to me has struggled with his own demons of addiction, which has sadly made him a non-participating member of our family for several years. I know he's endured an overwhelming amount of pain and suffering from his own relationship with Al. After a couple of near-death experiences, Mom, my siblings, and me resorted to an intervention encouraging him to turn his life around, because we feared losing him forever. This year, I had the opportunity to give my brother my thirty day sobriety coin. I've spent years praying for him to find peace. He told me he's working his own program and is earnestly trying to reconnect with our family. This summer, he met the kids and me at North Avenue beach, the same one Al had taken us to as kids. Just like Dad, he bought everyone ice cream. We swam in the lake, played football, and then, just like Dad again, we walked through the zoo. I was unable to hold back tears—for the sweet, fleeting memories and for the miracle of my sweet brother's recovery.

New Year's Day 2017, I received from my brother a sweet note. First of all, he alluded sardonically to Mom's "trickery" in intervening for his rehab, but he continued by expressing a heartfelt thanks to all of us for his six months of sobriety, expressing his joy in his strength to resist alcohol the past few holidays—including New Year's Eve and New Year's Day—despite running one of Al's restaurants with a mahogany wrap around bar! Inner strength, ya think?

God had winked at me—at us—again.

The cliche *hardships bring families closer together* has been true for us. Our parents gave us the most special gift in the world, *each other.* When we gather together, we tell stories mostly inappropriate in nature, and we laugh. We laugh a lot, and it always sounds like it feels so good, as though we realize we must cherish every moment, because such family klatsches are few due to clashes in the relationships. *It is the laughter we will remember . . . and the way we were . . .* sang Barbra Streisand almost fifty years ago, and memories are still vital for families. For a long time, I tried to mend the rend by confronting individuals and laying the conflict out on the table in hope of healing together. Today, I accept that I have not yet succeeded with that challenge. Since we returned to Chicago seven years ago, we try to host BBQ's, Thanksgiving, and Easter at our home. Some people show up, some show up late, and some never show up at all. My doors are always open, however, and come just as you are; all are welcome. I will never quit trying to bring us back together . . .

AL, REVISITED

Any positive interactions with Al have been few, but I am grateful for them. He went back to living above one of his establishments after the divorce and we see each other only a couple times a year typically prompted by a large group of us getting together for a celebratory event. He has healing of his own to do. My hope is he recognizes the importance he *could* play in the lives of his children and grandchildren and that I only want the best for him physically, psychologically, emotionally, and spiritually. Al had an emergency quadruple bypass surgery a few years ago and has Type II diabetes he badly manages. I had high hopes his medical emergency would bring us closer together. We all (including Fluff) rallied to help take care of him by delivering groceries, by sitting with him, by carting him to doctor's appointments, by shooting him with insulin and monitoring his blood sugar. As usual, he dashed my expectations, and I was crushed. People must desire change before it can happen. Nobody can force it upon anyone.

I've written Al many letters throughout life, always expressing my longing for a relationship with him, calling and leaving a message on his answering machine, or stopping by his apartment for a visit, but he's typically non-responsive. I've also tried to address vis-a-vis some of our conflicts, my sincere attempts always ending, however, in explosive arguments and months of *no-word-from* punishment. Consequently, I have needed *many* years of therapy myself for a balm in the wounds of this relationship. At thirty-eight, I can finally say that I have progressed from angry and defensive to sad and vulnerable. *I am at peace* in my journey with my father after arriving at a place called Acceptance.

MOM

Thank God for Mom. Fluff has been an inspiration and is the most loyal person I have ever known. She enjoys warm, close relationships with her grandchildren. They can not wait for the weekends she shows up at their soccer games, and they cherish movie and dinner dates with her. She supports my every endeavor, never judges or expresses negative opinions about anyone, grants everyone the benefit of the doubt and "accentuates the positive." Never have I heard her say a bad word about Al. *It takes two to speak the truth—one to speak, and another to hear,* according to Henry David Thoreau. Mom has helped me heal from many wounds simply by listening to and by appreciating my opinions, as though they were works of art, even when she disagreed with them, and even when I've been verbally insulting to her. She's gotten varying degrees of blame from everyone for leaving and *tearing our family apart.* I still stand behind her for the new life she created for herself like a phoenix from the ashes after the struggle with Al. On her sixtieth birthday, she gave my sisters and me a symbol of her love, a gold heart charm from a bracelet my grandma had bequeathed her. There's an engraving on the back from Grandpa to Grandma: *Merry Christmas 1966 Love Don.*

ME

Each time I sit down to write or to reflect, I reminisce about that brown faux shag carpet above the bar. I remember the carefree innocence of trolling roller skates through the neighborhood streets, of blowing Hubba Bubba bubbles, and of wearing out Nikes skipping along those same hot Chicago streets on my way home from school. I light a lilac candle, and I say a prayer while clutching Grandma's bracelet like a rosary between the fingers in my lap. I remember the smell of buttered popcorn making me feel safe; I return in my mind's eye to the race against Mr. T and to the victory validating my sense of self-worth. I revisit the time we all stuffed ourselves into the convertible Caddy and the crossbars gouged the backs of my legs. Oh, how I miss those times. All of us cherish poignant memories . . . but I must remember solemnly that I once had a dad. I pray hard to Mary, Mother of God for him. I tighten my grip on the bracelet. I remember walking into the bar, greeted by the regulars downing their usual, and glancing up at the hovering, vintage Schwinn, and then seeing Al across the room, happy. I will my legs to run to him, almost running in place at my desk, remembering.

He hugs me.

He tells me he loves me.

He tells me he'll see me later, at home.

I believe him . . .

. . . I believe in myself.

ACKNOWLEDGEMENTS

To my spirit animals, my miracle workers, my tribe:

Pauline Aguilera, Erik Powell Sr., and Lynn Rawden. Because of you,

this book came alive. I can't do anything alone. I am forever grateful

for your expertise, direction, and belief in this autobiography having

the capacity to change lives. Most importantly, thank you for the

beautiful friendship that evolved through this journey.

God Wink.